THE MANUSCRIPT

Chronicle 2

Panagiota Makaronis

KREA PREA

I dedicate The Manuscipt Chronicle 2, to my Late Father Constantinos Makaronis.
A contribution to his name for he was a noble and hard working man, that loved his Family and wanted the best for his kids.

He migrated in Australia from Greece in the 1960s'

Where he passed away in the hands of the corrupt, I could not of written this book without his experiences, where I had the privledge to live through it too. Where I get the oppurtunity to state my facts and leave a Legacy behind honouring his name.

GOD Knows what he went through. All I know he was a strong man, and he went through Hell fighting a lost cause!

R.I.P. BA BA!!

Νέος στην καρδιά γέρος στην ψυχή

Néos stin kardiá géros stin psychí

Translation;
Young at heart old at soul

KING OF PEACE!

CONTENTS

INTRODUCTION

The Manuscript is part two of the second coming, a follow-up from the 1st Chronicle, The Theatrical Melodia of my life. Initiated by my inner thoughts and my fighting spirit to cave in on a concept based on my own theories of how I perceive society. I have crossed many paths and skipped a few momentums, for I wanted to live to see another day I did not want to surrender by foul play or fall into a trap of procrastination.

What a sense of relief, when I realized I was just passing through, creating a temperament, while restoring my energy. Terrorized by the past, tempted by the views of those who assume hitting me and running will solve their issues, continuing their path soldiering on like I never existed.

While I was learning a lesson and creating a piece, I was being inspired by the spirit to release peace. During that whole ordeal, I could sense foul play, with a touch of adolescence and as Ideocracies go, I ceased to wonder why I reacted the way I did. Obviously, it had to do with power and the way the corrupt play it, it had me questioning their method all the way.

Leaving a poison in the atmosphere, where the world went into chaos and it handed me the energy to follow through and feed off the synergy. As I took that lie all with a stride, I counteracted with a few, and stirred the pot too, to get a reaction for inspiration. Because I needed to follow up on a dream lay the law, report those who were misleading me. No

1

longer have the power to trap pretend or connect in the end just redeem another conviction.

The assumption became an interruption handing them a foundation, to give them power to interpret and follow up on another destination. All I handed was a statement, a stream of events that messed up the concept but not my head. Because that method was a presentation to help me get ahead and harm those who were creating a war in my peace.

Returning later, releasing energy following up on another recipe, I had to remain consistent, a reminder that my fighting spirit was being tarnished. Where I refused to waste another day on a lost cause. For corrupt were caving in on the concept to get through, leaving me on the brink of having a nervous breakdown so they can achieve their goals.

What a scheme I had to undo before it took over my destiny right through, I needed to reestablish my point of view, read between the lines, and work at it at my own pace. Lining the corrupt up for another feast one where they no longer have the power to the peak. Planting a seed, left them stagnant, all so, I can succeed in lining them up for another feed.

Before I got caught up in another feast, I needed to return the favour, make sure there was no follow-up to that present day, that made my light darken and the corrupt shine all the way. I resented the fact I was pulled out of my comfort zone to save those who had no intention of giving me a chance of redemption. Allowing those who knew to govern my spirit, right through, was giving me half a chance to relive my destiny. The other half was handed to them periodically where my luck changed. I was ghosted and they were working in unison feeding me doubt.

I fell into a trap, what was considered bad then now, will be a normal trait in the future! It makes you wonder what the new norm will be in years to come from now!

Having said that a human mind is a powerful tool and if you know how to use it you can get more done in a minute you just need to feed your mind and body by keeping them active.

My method was a gamble and I tested my patience and got a taste of venom, well played, by whoever wanted to challenge my spirit all the way. I Hope the Manuscript Chronicle 2, kindly serves you well, for it is my inspirational piece, a key to sacrificing those lost souls that are dead to me!

CHAPTER 1

◆ ◆ ◆

A PIECE TO THAT FEAST THAT GRANTED ME A WISH TO RELEASE PEACE

It is time I returned the favour caused an effect then stated it. where the corrupt were about to eat their own words so I can get through. With an added trace, to test the patience of those who erase. No longer in the mission. They have been cut off, where the entrance will be based trial not doubt.

Those who wish to create a war in my peace, will return to repeat another forge. An end to stalling because I did not give in. They had one thing against me, the rumour. What they had was another feast one where I return and release for the conclusion was an illusional, deraigned method.

Creating the fusion, forming an Alliance of my own was an impossible task. It was creating a nest egg, from the present. A future event where it exceeded beyond the now and allowed me to breath somehow, what an entrance to that past incident that created the vast.

It gave me a chance to see I was heading towards a path of dead-end. A trap to track down the corrupt and give them another chance to counteract. Leading me to a destination that had no reservation, all it had was a constant reminder that I was following someone else's one-track mind.

That knot in my stomach was a desire, to hold on to that final key. Just to give the corrupt another chance to see. I was not going to help them get out of that mess. Returning on the condition I teach them a lesson and create a mass murder in their heads, just so I can get ahead.

Watch me return and delve into the internal bliss. The one that the corrupt created while I was trying to avoid entering the Abys. My return will dig so deep inside their soul revealing another way in. Just so I can continue to feed off the sin. What a waste of energy from within.

Where the only way out will be the curse that I created through the verse and reveal another killing spree. Where I get to be free from that intermission let go and follow up on another piece. One where I can return and release. because they went out of their way to silently create a violence.

One where I had no chance in hell of revealing another killing. Unless I entered their realm excited the same way and hand them nothing but a dead end in return all the way. Lucky for me I went through that final review and found a way to conceal, reveal their plan.

For it was next, arching them up for another conquest. Where this time it backfires and I get away as quickly as I entered. Feeding off the next of kin, returning the favour so I can win for the change. For the lie was taking over the truth and I could not get by unless I doubted them all the way.

I freed myself from another fall. I believed the thoughts in the back of my mind were indeed. A fact, where in the long run I will overcome a clue. I just had to follow it all through all while I trained my thoughts take an error and accept defeat, while living in terror then try to believe in myself.

What and emotional roller coaster, I experienced just to find pleasure; I had no choice but to follow the intention on the hope of creating redemption to those who were feeding off my resurrection. For what it was worth, what I assumed what I knew caused an effect.

It had me creating the wrong method, I was defective detecting the wrong clue. Just to keep up with the corrupt from recasting me. The only way I could survive the trauma, that was caving in on me, was undo. Then try not to track down those who harming me to get through.

Because fear took over, it had me stagnant and the only thing I had left was that four-leaf clover. I found it sitting in my Garden of Eden the one that was eaten through by the corrupts method. Where those who were not permitted, entered without my consent.

Just so they can return and compete with me again. This time around I had sweat in blood not tears for the foundation I once knew was a challenge I could not review. Unless I chased away the blues and stopped attacking those who assumed they knew.

It was less of a burden, to accept reality, because the dream at the time was less than a formality. I went out of my way to stop another creative challenge from reoccurring. Where I lost my true self trying to get out of a death threat that was not a dead end.

It was a novelty to give the corrupt a chance to uncover up another debt. One where they will free me until the end for it is time. I return get that free ride and follow up on another subdivision. The corrupts dead-end competition, where competing with me now will be what I call a final recall.

One where I can return get what I came for walk away this time leaving a curse behind. Reversing will be incriminating. Declining or even silently creep up on me again will be a thing of the past. They will no longer be able to pretend for my foundation became strong a sturdy.

Where this time I have the final revelation, there is no destination worth speaking of. What there was, had me looking for way, to follow up on a key. Where I can return late and hand the corrupt another way out. No way I was going to give them a chance to return and hit me in advance.

For I could hear them planning another failure, in advance. One where I have no chance what I had was another talent wasted so the corrupt can have their way. Where the only way out now is to give them hell. A chance to uncover another clue, one where I have the corrupt cornered to get through.

The rumours have changed, others have done worse for wear along the way. Where my name is no longer as tarnished if anything I hid varnished and then vanished. Return for another day to report repeat and reveal a gamble to the game. Holding the corrupt to contempt where I dissembled.

Faced my fear and followed the path to restoration and reservation. I knew if I let it go before time, that my presentation will be handed to me as a final review. On a silver platter, an award that I earned in due time, what a free ride to the other side.

Holding me hostage and keeping me outbound, was a kind way to repeat report and challenge the corrupt with a method. One where they no longer carry that declaration, to create another war in my peace. For I caught them in the act, just before they were about to release another feast.

I cut them off completely, I had no choice, conspiring to feed off my spirit then rejoice. Compel and control my every move every time they came near me, I was sorry. Terribly terrified of what was to come next, the only individual I had next to me, to keep me grounded was the thoughts in my head.

With those fears lingering, I could not think straight or look ahead I was being belted in the head. By those who knew and assumed they were ahead of me. Holding me back, was there way to get back on track. I had to Soldier on now with that clue, so I can continue to flourish read between the lines.

Not look back and decline another rhyme, or regret a trap because I am back on track. For that Contingency Plan was in motion. I could sense I was on a mission to cleanse and clear another hit. A dead end with a death threat that led me to a destination that gave me reservation.

A roll up to the next mission. Where I can get back on track and delete another turn of events. It that gave me the power to interrogate and initiate while the rest ventilate. What I did not know, did not make a difference in the end, I followed my route anyway my intuition fell in a trap of deprovision.

Where I looked easy, somewhat vulnerable, but in fact I was solid, saving myself from another unwanted test where others were summoning me to cash in. Carry the notion they could lure me back in on the condition they can re-enter and win another fight.

But this time around I caved in on that too and handed the corrupt a chance to confide in me so I can oust them gently. While letting them know in advance that their method is now in my hands. I have them both cornered here, for both energies turned against me.

I was living two worlds and neither of them served me the way they were meant to. So, I decided to enter their world on my own free will, get belted, for I had no choice. I had to prove my innocence once I did my wounds would heal, I can pick up where I left off no longer holding on to that grudge.

Where I could live and breathe independently, just to see what method clicks. Then I can return and personally feed off it. I knew I was on the right track but the way I felt was opposite. It was killing me, I started to become obsolete somewhat ready to delete.

I could not find a way to fight for the truth and still live my life in unison with my soul. I kept feeding off the wrong goal and it was leading me to destination where I caved in on the concept too soon. I nearly lost my life, trying to call the shots, when truly it was too easy to feed off the clues.

The corrupt were working in unison with the opponent. Every time, they won a fight they became pungent. What I called an instant melody to my energy, I ended up becoming a felony. If I followed my thoughts fully, I would be torn first and last one sudden move, I would be in trouble again.

Either way, it felt I was being trapped in a world where I hit another dead end. Pretending I was no longer my own friend I became my own worst enemy. It was preventing me from reliving my life and my destiny. Just to make sure the corrupt never have the power to create a down size to my energy.

I had delay and create a world where if they enter and harm me it will backfire. What I was feeding off was the symmetric clue, I became synthetic, my identity was lost and so was my veracity of life. I did not give up though, or give in, but something was tiring me up down.

It was not allowing to follow my crown of glory, there was an entity that was handing me the energy. It was holding me hostage but at the same time handing me clearage. Where I knew my life was about to fall apart again if I gave in to it too soon, it was the only way I could live in a society.

It made no sense to my sobriety. I was to continue to pause an effect and try to please myself. Then everything fell out of place and I ended up diving into a dead end to replace another debt. The corrupt kept feeding off the consistency, that left me lining up for a vindictive role.

Where I had no choice but to coincide with them and to hand them another role. All while put all the bad news aside, live my life on the concept I no longer have subdivide. While I retrace replace or even consolidate with a challenge to cave in on the concept and follow up on another case.

Whatever both parties did to create the piece there was no trace here, because I did my part, I hated it, but I had to go back and forth cleaning up the mess that was left behind, for that was the only way I could get through and no longer step on my pride in my prime.

Only to realize I was cleaning someone else's burdens. I loved to know how I got over it and how I lucky I was to get back on track deleting another fatal attack. Remind me where I went wrong so I can delete delay and create a better day.

Return anytime I please, for I got all worked up for one thing. That was to prevent another entity re-entering and holding me hostage again. On the condition I work against the corrupts, so called interlude. I could state it, whichever way I wanted, I was put in a position worst than imagined

I was deleting and delaying another vision from the ground up. Where this time and around, I got in, repeat report, and gave the corrupt a chance to read my thoughts, in between the lines in advance. That is when I felt the need change, I could, no questions asked no time wasted to replace it.

If they attempted to grasp in to my energy, I made sure I was covered in toxicity. Where they could not feed off me. When I had the freedom to state the facts, I did not recreate it the way it was traced, so I had to return repeat report, for that energy had given me an indication held me hostage.

I was a victim to a moulage an investigation where others who were causing the problem trying to cover it all up by framing me. Where he who caved in on me was an enemy. Where I had to scheme to create a new theme replace that key that was stolen off me.

As I continued to do what I was set to do, just to create a precedent. A happy ending to innocent response to cave in on the concept and trace that peeved. Following up on another case. For those who had assumed they had power to consume were about to get a final review. A dead end to that death threat, where they threw me of track for their own safety net.

CHAPTER 2

❖ ❖ ❖

FALLING IN & OUT OF A TRANCE OF CREATIVITY & SELF DOUBT

Where are we now? Let me tell you, who where and How; Living through hell, a method to help the corrupt consolidate with one another, to get out and finalise a clue. Creating an anomaly to see who is strong and clever enough to break my spirit and feed off the key a condition to continue to breed.

God help us all! Who are victims to the corrupts theme! If there is one thing I can admit is yes! At times I do like to stir the pot, but that is the only way I can recreate and follow up on another plot. A feast to prevent the then from ever re-entering and harming me again on this occasion not the next.

I doubt there would be a chance to revaluate or differentiate again. I caught them in the act of befriending and attempting another defence. For that method created nothing but love and hate effect. What a wall that was about to collapse just so the corrupt can open the gate from hell.

Then shut it because the ending was not what they were expending. A final case where they had to hand me the key to reliving my destiny heaving all while handing me a heavy heart about to lose my dignity. Where I stand to accumulate a feast, a method that handed me a free ride.

Where I knew I hit a cause an effect, fed up with that method that left me holding on to another debt. A certain case that was about to be erased. I had a taste of the corrupt and a fair share of what was about to come next. This time around there about to confess, while I get them to pay me out.

For the debt accumulated, it was Denying me access in a world I completed a mission delayed. For the corrupt had the power to compete. What they had is repetition without me, for my views counted not discontinued. I am out of my mind right now, trying to undo a vendetta.

The one where the corrupt had on me and my final review. For I hit the end of that tunnel and the light was not as bright as I thought. I realized I was in for another inning, where the only way I can get through was undo another clue. Where this time around it was not a gamble or a test.

I was humiliated, in the mission a natural habitual effect. The seed was planted long ago, just before I ventured out on my own. When I came out of that trance, I felt delayed and somewhat creating the wrong impression that is when I knew I hit a depression.

All I wanted to do, was entertain my spirit and follow up on another clue. Where the other side was brighter somewhat kinder. I will no longer be wondering what I did wrong, what to do to get through. I know now who was in on it, what they were planning to do next, where to go from here.

Just to finally suppress another guess. For I caught them red handed, trying to feed of my innocence again, then get back in and succeed. With what feedback? I had nothing positive to say in the end I was tricked traced repeat a dead end, a taste of a medicinal phase leaving me totally disgusted.

Now I know, that the free ride was a no show. It was a challenge to give those who had the upper hand. A chance to apprehend another trend, then given power to get back on track and devour. Reminding me of the past event that was hovering over my head.

It was leaving me of debating of how to play it next. An avenue of a whole lot of unnecessary requests. Where I had to follow my route retrace another doubt paying out a debt or two, so when I reached my pinnacle. A position I could not review, unless I handed the corrupt another insight.

I had to follow my route, a condition to screw the corrupts mission all so they never re-enter. Trap me again and steal another clue. For the presentation had a final review, I had to replace an old thought with the new. One where the corrupt cannot re-enter and refuel.

Unless again they pay me out what they owe from the last cancelation. Because they prejudged me where it caused a revivification. Where I was to be paid out considerably. Now that I am here conditioning another vision, paying me out will be a better proposition.

For the debt accumulated and the only way to agree was to disagree. By entering and entertaining that method a follow up on another feast a prize-winning case would release. where no one else has the power to undo but me. This time around I am done calling the shots and creating a piece.

Just to keep the corrupt balanced, I might as well let it go and finalise another go. Where the corrupt no longer have the power to repeat report or rummage through another portal. What I had to do to was shape up and ship out and leave the corrupt in total doubt.

Out with the old in with the new and relying on only myself to get through too. Where all I got in return was a final review one with the indication that I would be followed towards the Abys where I get a chance push the corrupt in and watch them go through hell from within.

No longer I failing a thing, but I did get pushed in the corner belted to death in spirit and had to go back pick up where I left off on the hope the corrupt stop and think before they re-enter and peak by using me as a lead to the next stampede. No longer continuing to flourish to get back on track

No longer stuck tracing another hack. For that presentation was a given and the path I was on was on a relapse, a phase where I stumbled and fell into a trap. To get back on track and rebel against my free will to survive another skill. Where I was handed a key to stop the corrupt on their tracks.

Before they re-entered and handed me a follow up to the next phase. One where their presentation lined me up for an outcome where they kept me facing another hold up a frail moment where the key became final retrace where if I did not tread carefully, I would fail and fall into a trap of denial.

I was destined to keep up with the programme, regardless of how things had panned out, I was not aware I hit a trend, a trap a challenge where if I failed, I would have to go back and repeat delete delay and prevent another bad day from re-appearing.

But I realized I was being traced challenged cheated on and all I had to erase a condition. Where the corrupt had repetition to return and repeat. Where if they failed the first meet I et in and retrieve everything. Where the only way to get them out was to hate me again.

Have them turn against me instinctively, so when I return, I can feed off them internally. Leading them to a destination where their freedom will be cut short, until they repair the damages. The one that was created in my piece so I can return and find peace.

For the corrupt were trying there hardest to condition me and feed off my harvest. Meanwhile I was on the case restoring my energy releasing synergy. Where the only way they could take control and throw me off track was finalising another go. While I was trying to recreate relocate that final path.

For the path I was on was relinquishing another time bomb. A creative one lining me up for another outcome. For I wanted to make my world a better place for me to live peacefully, but I kept falling in to a trap of self-doubt, for there were naysayers trying there hardest to throw me off track.

Where I was put in a trance a provisional a development to get back on track and reinvent myself, little did I know I was led towards a destination of dead ends with death threats. The only way to set it free was carry it to the next destination and put the corrupt through such a dilemma.

Where the only time to restore me was to hand them a taste of that vision with an intervention individually. Then take it away from them with the notion I hand them a germ. A final revelation with caution no promotion or a boost of energy to sacrifice another synergy.

I was put on a path of restoring another yearning, where I carried that piece to the next desirable feast, a challenge I could not release. Unless I caved in on the concept and retrained myself from recreating a cheat sheet. For I had no time rehearsing a crime or revealing the truth to the corrupt.

Because I was hit with an odd thought in the back of my mind. What I was to do next and how to replace it without uncovering another mistake to that hostile moment was a regret. A less visible momentum to that vision that handed me proposition, where the result will clear the mission.

My head was bombarded to many thoughts, where I can look ahead. Feeding off the condition without leaving a trace behind. Where I fell in a trap, monitoring those who assumed they had all the answers. what I had was a chance in advance to follow up the outcome feeding off the income.

A challenge to create a piece where I can release and turn the events around to my favour and create a second chance, where I can forward and oust those who are in the corrupt out of my world. Straight into a destination where they cannot erupt or trap trace or give in to the end of the race.

This time around they no longer have the energy or the motivation to strap me up. Cause an effect or challenge me, what they have now is a momentum to recreate a follow up. So, I can move forward with entertainment and the prediction that never came into fruition.

I did nothing remotely that bad to deserve such an enormous loss of faith, hope or trace all I wanted was complete my tasks complete my mission and create another proposition to that division. Where the race ended way to soon, trying to persuade me to do something else.

A trace I could not erase, unless I fell out of that trance. All so they can return trap my energy with toxicity. Attempting to steal another key and wrapping me up in a problem, having me challenging it as I was tracing it. What a difference a day made though, for all I had to do was sleep on it.

Not sweep it under the carpet, for that created more germs, a generic effect that stated the wrong facts. An energy that crept up on me and left me entertained by the notion that I was stalling. But in fact, I was using them to face another decade, a challenge I could not have gotten out of on my own.

Unless I was in a coma, for the way it panned out it gave me a chance to delegate. Then finalise another time out, it felt as if I was comatose. For the road, I was on had me enlisted for another hit and run. Where I had to go relive it a present effect a presentation with another lift.

I had no time for that drama the trace was case less likely to be erase. Unless I caused an effect, return, cleaned up the mess and call it a day. Where I can back up get back on track, trace trick and drop another day to create a gamble to that scam that led me to a destination.

A presentation of dead-ends and death traps a denial that

19

went a mile. A bomb shell to that held me up and created a road a trip, a trap and trip, that tricked me down memory lane. A test I could not reveal, unless I tricked those who assumed they can return and face me, by stealing another clue.

Where this time around I found them entertaining and somewhat offensive. Where an opportunity arose and the only way, I could repeat return stir the pot and then delete it, just to oust them out. for I had the Midas touch I went to extremes to pass tests, lining them up for a conviction.

Just to feed their addiction. The only way I could get my foot in the door was challenge the corrupt all the way. Where this time around I cornered them on the condition I face my fears. Follow them until the end where the result will be a dead end for them a free ride for me to survive.

I had work to do working overtime to screw those who knew and undo those who had a clue. For I had no time for fun or games the respect was long gone. It created a dead end to those who were not my friend what they were, and will always be our enemies trying to befriend me again.

Where throwing me of track hit them with a vengeance. Seen as I saved them the least; they could do was repay me with the same old trend a trace until the end. On the condition that they cancel that method that created a piece, that left me delaying another release and hand me the way out.

No more causing effects on the condition they resurrect, lead me to a destination of a defect. Where I can return and follow up on another phase a top end race. Handing me a challenge, one where the corrupt will have no choice but to reveal another fluke.

A topic that raises awareness, a condition based on repetition. The one that was created when I was going through revision. An added feast in the back of my mind ready to repeat. I had to stay alert just to reduce another trace get back on track and erase.

Leaving the corrupt deleting delaying and feeding off each other. Just so I can get back on track and further. No more doubt in my mind either, for that feeling that I once had, where I doubted myself. worried what others thought, no easy way out, I no longer wanted to carry that uncertainty.

It was caving in on me, for I was handing others opportunity to hit me run, and call it a day. I was not aware I was victim of despair, where others assumed I was there cover up. No more I am about to uncover it all on the condition I no longer fall. put in a position of playing a game of truth and dare.

Declaring myself insane, so the corrupt can return repeat report a follow up on another claim. Handing them that pain so I can continue my path. For it is time they case close it and follow another route, a clean way out of that race that handed me a cold case.

Where the outcome was all, I needed to finalise another meltdown, one where I handed the corrupt that clue on the condition, I can feed off them right through. For the next time, they re-enter it will be on my conditions not theirs, where they will have to pleasure me continuously completing it all.

No choice in the eye of the beholder either, for that is what caused the effects it created a moulder. For that method was old news, it rotted away and the only way out was to pull it out and clean it up. Handing the corrupt doubt right in the middle of a test, they were middle eastern.

Mediterranean not Asian descent. Where they must give into me before they hit an invasion to that destination. For the pressure was way too harsh to contest, where another route was about to come out to fruition. With the notion they assumed they were winning; in fact, they were scheming.

I was playing it purely to get in and harm them from within. Because they used me, brought me forward and then again turned against me. Making me believe I was to blame and out to be a liar a cheat a user and abuser. It was well played, turned against me, so I can go through hell on purpose.

It got to the point, I gave in spaced out and handed the corrupt no ammunition to fight back. I kept my mouth shut for too long I pleased them I had no choice they locked me shocked me from within with disbelief. I Went behind there back created a piece returned the favour, so I can release peace.

The unlimited ammunition was a conviction to feed the corrupt their addiction. Where working against them was the only way, I can get back on track and press replay. I was feeling the punch of another inning a creative sense without a second chance to repent.

What a dead end to that death threat a condition that caved in on the mission. It handed me repetition, given me a chance to see I hit a cross road. It was causing effects, trying to delete my vision, no longer in the mission. A final review to shock those who fell in a trap of leading me on.

Towards a destination where they can stay strong, a

THE MANUSCRIPT CHRONICLE 2

challenge I could not revive. For my silence was killing my survival technique. I had to reverse that course feed off that that verse. Then hand the corrupt a poison to their vision, all so I can get back on track and complete my mission.

Where I no longer continue to sit in self-pity and review another Whitty momentum. For it would have become a decade of trying to prove my innocence. Lucky for me I did not have to play it, nor did I have the time try to prove my innocence, I decided to pay out that debt.

On a condition the corrupt pay for it in mind body and spirit, Soul searching for eternity. They are punished, live in a life time of neglect regret and constant doubt in the back their mind. All while I continue to flourish, strive with no dead end nor death threats in sight.

My mind clear with the reminder I hit a hold up to. Trying to complete a task that I could not finish, when asked. I was constantly on the move being challenged to clear else's fight. A point of view kindly telling me what to do, is now my way to breathe right through.

I am done pretending that the feast was pending a foundation needed mending. For all along I was being targeted. Stirred, deliberately pushed to my limits so the corrupt can continue to live on the edge and hand them a dead end with constant death threats in the head.

What a liar they made me out to be so they can continue be free. Hitting a mind reading hold up. So, I can get ahead survive, he who was in harm's way; then get out of his way. For it was a lie, just for the truth to get by. Once I got through the rest was ancient History a thought based on a fantasy.

As I follow my path until the end of the day, I will accept

what comes my way. What a wrong move on their end though, where everything now has hit a happy ending. a free ride for me to kindly say goodbye. I am done having my leg pulled, for the corrupt to keep strong every step of the way.

Only time will tell, time to wait and see you might as well continue your path then lead the way. The rest will have to pray because I am done laying the law every step of the way. I am individual with the ideas and notions of my own accord; my experiences given power to return and devour.

They taught me well, how to live breath silently retrieve, see society to what it is. Where my conviction was based on a conclusion, a challenge that served me well in the end of that trend. Made me see I was too busy fighting for a lost cause that clearly was no longer meant for me.

Where it will remain until the day I am gone! Where my spirit will live on. A cleanse, where I could not erase or finalise a review to get through, a method where I found myself heaving at justice. Just to give the corrupt a chance to face me in advance and hand me another clue.

CHAPTER 3

❖ ❖ ❖

LINING ME UP FOR A KEY THAT SAVED ME

All while holding my spirit to ransom, creating a piece. Giving me a chance to release and find peace. It got to the point I had to set it free, pressure my spirit to claim another one for me. So, when I reached the next level, I could sense that the mission hit a disposition, restore my energy.

Accept repeat report rely on myself and then delete it. I had to rule out all that was holding me back, because my possibilities were limitless. I had several who wanted to push me of track, challenge me with obstacles and release a demon to cancel out another vision.

Lining me up for another cancelation key to have me

uncover up a challenge. For a competition not worth revisiting, arose. I might as well revamp continue my path not look back just forward, create a piece to lift my spirit and bring peace.

I had to rely on my own self-worth to release. Not expect to get a thing in return from anyone. For I had to follow a certain way, for those who were taught by the system also had to retrain. Follow a certain rule, and protocol, where if they do not follow the rules, it will hand me power to compete.

One false move on their end, they lose their control and recognition. Where I get back on track cheating on the system and recreating another violation to that destination. No longer have the strength to follow up on another trend trace trap or give in to another feast.

Where they can undo and prevent me from living my destiny. For the only way to condition it was hand me the key so I can hand them permission to no longer continue to feed off the mission. because I wish to undo that association. It had me following the wrong path.

Feeding those who had to lead to get back on track succeed by tracking me down. Pushing me towards the wrong direction and then lying about me. In the end of the whole saga, it had me on a third trial. Violating my destination that created the proposal that had me at a point of no return.

The only way I could return was rebuild, establish a condition to hand me repetition. A promise that was not kept silent from me, making me believe I was safe. The facts they were killing me even though I knew it I could not change it unless I recreated in an instant thought.

The method backfired and left me resenting everyone who was hired to keep me held up. It was creating a war in my peace just to hand them another chance to release and conspire. A limitless effect a reaction of death threats. An advance, to release peace to resist an ending that was pending.

Lining me up for failure so they can resign and leave me deleting then denied access. Feeding off the concept instead of living it the way it was meant to. I let it all go cornered attacked and left to suffer; I was conned with a fake a proposal. A task impossible to achieve unless I was less than human.

So, I created a piece revealed another feast, put the corrupt through hell. So, I can get back on track a prepare myself for another trace. Where this time if they return and hit me when I hit my summit. Where their method will collapse and I will get back on track with the same old lap dance.

Little did I know I was being taught a lesson, for what reason only time will tell. In the end the concept was intrusive and those who were in on it were elusive. Waiting for me to fail at every chance, giving me a hard time so I do not reveal their angle.

For it was creating a personal vendetta. Wearing a mandala that was stating the facts, but not giving me the chance, I needed to react for that passion that was leaving me feeding off the poison. A trace a trap to make sure the corrupt get away with hitting me and running and end the race sooner.

Strangling me at every passionate momentum, leaving me all chocked up. I had troubles getting through it got to the point, I felt myself falling into a trap where it was a holding me up. It gave me the indication that they were heading to a path where every time I hit my pinnacle, I was frail.

I could not fight back or prevail it was leading me off track. I was feeling the pressure the pain and the anxiety. Every time I got back on track to chase the blues or free myself from another clue, something sinister will show its ugly head. Facing me with another dilemma with a death threat.

A final review to kindly finalise, then present the corrupt with a feast. Just to hand them a challenge to release. Where the competition was creating repetition, and the corrupt were on a mission to heave at me again and the only way I could cancel another value was cave in on the system.

Then prevent the corrupt from ever returning and heaving at me again. For every time they faced me, they held me hostage took me in followed my route. Pressured me to cause an effect, then return to show its ugly head and hand me doubt all over again.

All I had was a time out to repeat report and delete a leading proposition. But at the spurt of the moment, I was torn in two worlds. I had to cleanse hold myself up and not allow the corrupt to re-enter and help me get back up, no longer holding me to contempt.

Because the foundation was pending and my validation intertwining and the only way I could play was to agree to disagree and the rest would be History. Having said that my vision was impaired and my foundation no longer in the mission of caving in on the intuition.

For I could sense that I was being prepared for an entrance a trace added with a vengeance. Where I got a chance to feed off that mission and prevent the corrupt from ever re-entering and handing me another proposition. I had to heal from the past live in the present and look forward to the future.

I was being haunting and I could not think straight unless I accepted defeat and allowed it to no longer hand me anguish. I was afraid I would fall into a trap of addictions, a trace I could not reveal unless I trapped those who decided to re-enter and finalise everything to their favour.

Leaving me causing effects and handing luck while they were preventing me from ever reliving mine. I was pressured to push them in the corner and prevent them from ever re-entering my holy grail. for letting them in will hand them another win living in a condition instead of a vision.

Not worth reliving not well said or done. Just hand them an outcome, where I would end up failing everything, with no time to go back and forth just lie to myself so they can continue to flourish. I fed of the maze as they continued to nourish off me preventing me from reliving my destiny.

For what I had was not my expectations it was a final feast to get back on track and release peace. Prevent the corrupt from ever tormenting me with that lease that handed me that feast. Where I could not retrace unless I follow that pace and prevent them from ever reopening another case.

Because the past was an open and shut one, the present was a cancelation between them and what was to come next. Where if I was not careful, I would be caught up in a web of lies. Denying myself truth and value while giving the corrupt a chance of salvation.

All while they were handing me starvation. Desperate for a chance for a last a final trial, where the future endeavours for many had changed. Several lost, many won during that line up effect. but those who were in the middle could not finalise a thing unless I gave in.

For it was not in the mission or stable because the present and the past was a Fable and I got a chance to prove my innocence in advance. It left me caving in and lying to myself so I do not lose my soul so when I reach my pinnacle, I could not breach another trace.

Because I had to return and erase, following up on another case. The last resort ended up cynical and my method had me reliving a challenge. Pending, until I came up with an outcome to pressure and push the corrupt in the corner. Handing me what they owe me with recognition.

Deposition and leadership, I could not undo until I accepted, the fact that I was lied to. To get through was a challenge. It was enough for me to see I was being stalked by those who lacked energy and they needed to feed off to save themselves for absurdity.

The whole concept became strange after the fact, I felt the whole outcome change. I fell out of place, where everything was too good to be true so I decided to let it go and feed off the no show. Where opportunity arose, I got in fair and square and my last and final recall.

Lined up with a hold up, a final review to hand me the title. A key that was stolen off me. Where I fell out of that trap on the other end, trying my luck to comprehend. lining the corrupt up for a challenge where they can no longer conceal. Unless I create a feast to that piece where I retraced it.

Stalled to see where to hit next then return the favour to recreate a protest. Just to clear and cleanse another debt.

Lucky for me no one really knows what the future holds, the world changed and so did the energy that created the piece, but never did any one see it coming.

Nor create the forthcoming, the way it was meant to because it was too easy to decipher. There was no way I was to retort to the old way of thinking. I had to return to my cunning ways no longer relive the drama and empower every step of the way.

When you sense energy creeping up on you, its visibility becomes a clue. You know for you are being warned, there is a drama or two about to come to fruition. You can feel its presence, taking a step back waiting to see what the outcome will be, will hand you the indication.

You are about to hit another confirmation. That is when you know it is there but you cannot see it, where it can lead, you to destination you cannot leave freely. Unless you change the whole concept. Assumptions have a habit of taking over your spirit an indication you are harm's way.

The fact was you were being warned to get saved from be sworn at. Finally, when you get there, you can end up in a worse for wear if you do not take a moment to undo that despair. That energy left behind caves in on you. Staring at you waiting for the right moment to make it happen.

Where you procrastinate; If you are not careful you will never be ready. You will end up sorry, with a never-ending story. I became a saw loser in my own world, a follow up to the new world. Where the old world was challenged with the notion, they had the power to take over my free will.

Where I was stuck and struck by a middle eastern lie. In the middle of a test a trace a trap and a drop to the next contraption. Corruption took over and I had to figure out how to get out. All by having them work side by side. A trick to give the corrupt a chance to rekindle a relationship with me.

With someone new, because now I know what to expect. I outgrew and finalised another clue and gave the corrupt a second chance for me to give in and state the obvious and that was game over check mate. That was the only way I could free myself from that gamble that handed me the clue.

Stalled long enough for me to get through. I can return and feed off the west leaving north and south feasting of the rest. For that drama that caved in on was a presentation revealing another key that had become a dead-end idling until the end.

The only way to challenge me from within was prepare me for the worst. Because the worst was to about to begin and all I had was a foundation with a reservation full of dead ends and death threats. A challenge I had no chance of reliving, for this time around I had to face a fear.

No one was giving me opportunity to face me because they knew if I faced it, I would erase it. So, I found my trace, trapped tricked the corrupt to replace me with another key, where this time around I return to hand them a glitch. A clash where they cannot latch on to me even if they tried.

In the end it became worse for wear wearing un undergarment on their heads. One to cover their mouths to keep the germ out. From expressing their eternal bliss and leave a matter of fact to the feast that gave me the power to release peace.

A trap that gave the corrupt another chance to counteract and hand me a counterfeit melody, a soundwave that caused an effect that left my personality cold hearted. Where it had me caving on in on the concept, with the intention of never seeing light at the end of the tunnel ever again.

My mind was made up I had no choice but to cause an effect of my own and hit the corrupt with a creative delegation. Where if they re-enter on the condition of cornering me and forcing me to close one door and handing them another key. On the condition they no longer read me.

But this time around they feed me. The chance they once had to re-enter and explore will be a gamble at their own risk. For their foundation was a trace to feed off the case and cancel that race. Before they got a chance to re-enter and prevent me from ever seeing the truth.

Whatever was holding me back was a method, created by piece. It threw me off track solved nothing, for those who were in on it were about to get a taste of their own poison. For that reason, there was treason in between where this time around, I ignored the truth.

Followed my route let them in by wearing rose Coloured glasses. Where they will see the truth and those choices that were made during that time. I was going through that maze, an entertainment to hand them a follow-up to next restoration.

 Because the test was a feast and the rest was concept where the only way. They could follow it through was take a challenge and if I passed it the rest is history. For it was not the conclusion that created the piece, it was the challenge, where the trace became a presentation.

Where that method was about to be released. I had no time to prove my innocence because what ever happened was a repeat and all I had to do was accept defeat. It was the last and final review for me to cash in and follow another route, to the next destination.

Where I found a good reason to prevent the corrupt from ever repeating another treason. For their plan to hunt me down haunt me again with a passive aggressive approach. It was about to back fire and that method will have its faith changed challenged and cheated on.

The only way to contaminate will be the follow up to the next trap a trace that will give me the power to erase and trace those who empower so when I get back on track, I can devour another vendetta. I was perceived, by those who had the freedom to contaminate.

It gave me the energy that I needed to take control of my soul. The only way I could get the energy I needed to explore was repeat a bad day. Handing me the indication I was on my way. It took me back to an environment, where I could state a new fact a follow up on a treatment.

It left me poisoning the corrupts method back-to-back. Taking that final cold case and revealing another cover up. A trace to erase piles up on the next case, no longer postponing because I made it to the next donning. While I feed off that pace, reminiscing about the past in the back of my mind.

I could sense reality was about to decline. I started to daydream and instead of following that path I was working against my own free will. Just to cave in on the concept for I was about to give in and hand them everything without knowing. It gave me the indication that I was about to hold up.

Repeat another starvation while holding on to the next

cast. Where this time around I have the upper hand. I found myself no longer looking for answers, for that perception had me in the middle of my vision. A light shining in my peripheral vision, a revelation to keep me honest.

Where the corrupt a chance to feed off that cause an effect all so I can hand them a dead-end. A destination with a final bashing before I reach my accreditation. A condition creating an entity, where my energy will send me to a place where I am safe.

For those who were in on it will be cornered, until further notice. For it is time, they paid for that final review a case to shut and review. Meanwhile they open another secret passageway one I can only see so I can get through periodically so I can resolve my issues mentally.

The only way for them to escape, will be there grave, whatever they did to make this hold up occur. A challenge to reveal another kill. I had no idea I was about to cave in on the method and shock those who decided to enter skip a venture an avenue that was leading me to an adventure.

I was being used and abused thrown off the edge holding onto a final cast. Just so the corrupt can continue to blast me with an outcome from the past. Starve me while they compete leaving me feeding off the mission and repeating another disposition.

Cursing the problem was not the answer, avoiding it was though, just so I can get my act together on the condition I follow my route and release another doubt. I was restoring, getting back on track, and reveal another fluke, what a revelation I had, just by revealing the truth.

Leaving the corrupt doubting me while I continue my path. A follow my route to the next craft. A trace to trap and challenge that method so I can reveal a feast to that piece. I return to cause that effect, get back on track and resurrect, leaving the corrupt struggling in the middle of a test.

Pushing me from one end to the next, creating a conquest. Leading me to destination reserving another competition. A free ride to the other side, where I had no time to waste or wait for the other one to experience that preservation. A provision to end the work, of he who is not civilised.

CHAPTER 5

◆ ◆ ◆

THE INCREDIBLE LIE THAT GAVE ME THE POWER & THE SECOND CHANCE TO GET BY

I went through it all and before I was to repeat, time I let it go, rely on what I know and move on. On the condition I stay strong. Follow my route on the hope I keep up with the programme with no doubt in mind without a siren to warn me I was about to become deranged rearranging a clue.

Meanwhile being declined again, a harsh reality, too late to create a world of love. Surrounded by so much hate. Whatever I did to repeat a scheme it was all based-on a past event. Back load of unfinished business in the mist. Where I was lied to by those who knew and those who had a clue.

I was not being productive it was causing an effect, having others trying their best reverse. Then have burst out in flames so they can continue to come first. It was restoring my energy handing me a clue so I can get through. Feasting off my spirit cash in, delay delete then hold the corrupt hostage.

 So, they no longer return and repeat for their own selfish reasons. So, they can overcome can over estimate and overindulge in another iconic momentum. Where they sacrifice my spirit and lead me to a destination where I harm myself. Just to get a chance to relate and harm me in advance.

Where it left me deleting and delaying everything again, it was what it was, and I was on the mission but it would have been an impossible task for the lie to create the piece or give the corrupt another chance to get by and release.

I decided to repeat another hit, put myself through that trace again just so I can return and teach them a valuable lesson. On the condition I give the corrupt a chance to erase and clear that repetition that was giving me definition. a debt to start off with when it comes to debts;

The corrupt like to weasel out of it, they do not like to pay, but they do like to play. There mood changes when they caught, they become suspects, making you, their victim. Their method is changeable, they relinquish grief so you lose and they win, a non-win situation on bother ends.

A chance to create piece was a free ride to the other side they will do anything to harm those who are not there yet to get in and try their luck while they continue to return and recreate a war in your piece. Feeding off you at every trace a case that served me well and hit me in the end of that spell.

What a challenge I had to release in the mist of it all to find peace so I no longer fall back or fall out of place just keep up with the programme hounding the corrupt at every destination. Attempting to kill their spirit from within a method to have me cave in on the concept and follow up on a feast.

Where they assumed I was the weakest link and they had the power to trace trap and trick me into thinking otherwise. Because I hit a dead end, I was threatened assuming they had the power to keep me down by those petty threats that left me caving in on the system.

Breaking my spirit and lead me to a destination where I am full of regret. Lacking peace persistence and leaving me restoring someone else's energy. Where my outcome was beyond repair, no positive thought was going through my mind either, I had a lot of issues to deal with.

The main was way too intrusive to declare or decline. Letting go was difficult too, because I was purely lining myself up for a dead end and a death threat to get another clue. It was holding me to contempt giving me a challenge, I could not comprehend.

Where I had a free ride to lead me to a destination, where I had to return. Then hand the corrupt a chance to pretend and reveal a failure in advance. Pending with a vengeance waiting to steal their thunder, cleaning up their method sealing the deal while being warned in the back of my mind.

I was about to fall into a trap, where I am to travel against all odds. Pretending I have nowhere to be, but back where I started in the middle of a steep edge. So sharp, that if I was not careful, I would be cut so deeply the wound would be worse for wear.

Leading me to a destination where I had no conclusion just

the resolution to claim another composition that will hand me the conditions based on a repetition that handed dark cloud over my vision. For the next trace will erase a follow up on another pace neglecting the facts.

I had to get back on track, by returning and relaying messages to those who knew. For they assumed they could steal another clue, overlooking the truth was the only way they could get through. Pretending I did not exist, was not part of the mission but it was a proposal to get the approval.

I needed to return and follow up on another term, all by causing an effect. Challenging that one descendant from ever reliving, because they inspired me to carry on to the next division. Creating a piece to send me packing for I did my part, played the game, and got nowhere, it drove me insane.

A cleanse to claim a fellowship to the next composition was enough for me to see I was free riding and counting the waves to reach the other side. I needed to prevent the corrupt from ever re-entering and claiming another conviction, for it was a forethought.

A deception to reclaim return another key to validate and infuriate those who come and gone. While consolidating with another by returning to reveal a yearning. It got to the point I had no free time, what I had was certain individuals causing effects.

Feeding off that presentation so I can get back on track and reserve another validation. For they were looking for a feast to piece together and release. a thought that left me revealing another shocking revelation. Where I had to return storm through a passion retrace another conviction.

A trip down memory lane, where my condition was based

on my personal vision. Where I had to recreate another path, get back on track down load the energy to those who reported me. Then and repeat another trap. This time around I am not depending on anyone.

Where if I fall, I get back up and rise above it all, because when you depend on others, you run the risk of you needing them. Where if they do not return, you run the risk of feeding off them, where it gives them the power to take over your will and leave you sucking up to them.

A rude awakening, where they solemnly never return anyway, why would they? A concept that was creating a piece gave them what they wanted leaving it to the imagination. On a condition I feed them a whole lot malarkey then present them with debt a chance to return and resurrect.

That method that handed them favours back when, has now subsided, there is no vision or competition what there is, is another outcome a competition to hand me the revision. For I needed to return, conclude what went wrong cleanse my spirit, to stay calm grounded strong.

My freedom had handed me a piece to create a validation form a foundation feed off that contest and release. Where I was about to be handed a personal vendetta a final review to cave in on the concept and prevent the corrupt from re-entering.

Because at the beginning they handed me the wrong vision, disguised themselves as friends but in fact they were enemies' rivalries returning for a demonic inquisition by terrorising my intuition. All while I released followed up on a feast, a conclusion to dictate and then indicate what to do next.

How to get them out of my head? Then return for another feast putting them through a collage to release peace. Then collect memorabilia to hand them nostalgia. Putting them through a dimension, where the curse cannot be reversed. Unless I set a precedent and match to light another fire.

Where the corrupt took a gamble, based on a scheme where I had nowhere useful to turn. But back to that final review a feast I cannot see unless I hand them another key. For this time around I am algae here, clouded, tormented by the present the past and what the future may hold.

Where my thoughts take over and unfold another feast to that piece that created a scheme. One where I could not release unless I lived that lie. For that free ride was no longer in the mission time went by the interpretation, I had was the lie; it served me in the end of that forthcoming spell.

I had to create a truth to it, for that scrutiny left me hitting a final review. Allowing it to eventuate by stating it. A curse where I had to return the favour to the sender. Where the only way to do that was hit the messenger, and not return to milk it for all its glory. For the guilt was worse that the hit.

What for, I had no time for another crime, so I decided to frown upon it. Create a piece and make sure I no longer make mountains out of mole hills. Trying my hardest to stop handing the corrupt a chance to harvest, while I was going through the whole glory trying to convince myself otherwise.

Then cave in on the system so I never have to unfold or free the story untold, until I hit the mile stone. I knew that energy was trying to cast a spell, a trace to trap terrorises, those who cancel and class that act with a feast to praise release to those who don't deserve to find peace.

Where if I played it to soon, I would be denied access and handed anxiety right through. Knowing where it came from would not of made a difference. I had to go through the emotional blackmail that was caving in on me, it was preventing me from living my life, reveal revoke then revolve a lie.

Handing me a condition that was lining me up for another competition. Going for the kill was the only way I could reform and fail those who had the entertainment. Just to create an energy that was harming me in symmetry. A conspiracy to attempt to case close then harm me.

Before I had a chance to cave in on the concept in advance, a challenge they could not deny. For I was not there yet and the only way for me to get in. Present them with a clue so they can do what they set out to do. On the condition I can return once I get there and cancel it all out.

Leaving them handing back those keys, they stole of me including my thunder. Just so I can retrieve and achieve another trace, a repellent to that repeat that was handing me the wrong key. Keeping up with the program was an emotional blackmail I could not see beyond; a life time sentence.

While I was revealing another truth, creating a clue, poisoned by the system. Where the repetition became an incursion. Leaving the spirit to intervene start a fight, cave in on the concept and trap those who knew, corner them. Just to get that spurt of energy, that was handing me regret.

Holding me to contempt creating an anomaly while

feeding off the interval. That made my spirit assertive while trying to push me out of regression. Just to get that decision that will hand me the light in the long run in the meantime. I had to fight, a dilemma just to reach my potential.

Without having to kindly review and harm those who knew. for I had to flee, before I had a chance to be me. Condition that pathway towards a destination I can relate to, so when I hit a home run where the outcome will be based on one clue. Feed off that trace hand the corrupt a new pace.

A challenge I wish to preach, shock those who solemnly swear, have the audacity to return and scare me to death. For it gave me the power to prevent the corrupt from ever reliving another dream on my second trial. The plan was to cause an effect and harm me within every challenge.

Where my method was being tarnished, where I had to run and hide. Just to prove I was innocent while those who were guilty were omniscient. I had to play it, to get through, for every time I hit the end of the journey, and start to reach my potential challenging the next.

I had to bail out to cave in on the concept for they kept threatening me with an external precision. An internal condition that left me afraid to follow up on my intuition. The only way, where I could get out of that personal vendetta safe and sound was runaway.

Find solidarity in solitary, a place where I can rest my head and get ahead, and please myself all the way. Where no one could re-enter and harm me in my centre of Harmony. A place I call home a safety net in the peripheral vision of my mind to carry on to the next and final repent.

A debt that paid out that death threat that was holding me to contempt. Not look back, just forward pray one day something good would come up and I will get to play anyway. Live that trace that I was creating through peace, not have to feel trapped in a world where it could have damaged me.

If I allowed them to play it their way, enter my realm fail me that way. So, I left that bad hand, the one faith handed me behind, where it created a feast to challenge the corrupt so I can release peace. A place where it belongs, and that is not in my vicinity.

Where the method was a trap to challenge me. Counteract fight back and hand the corrupt another chance to feed off me. Where I no longer must stand in trial, try to push forward while I am in denial for, I made it until the end. Fed off the concept cleansed my spirit and gave myself a chance.

Just to reveal another dead end in advance, prove that I was innocent. All by presenting the corrupt with a challenge, where their voyage was not set in stone and that presentation becomes invalid. When those challenges cave in on your perception you tend to feed off your intuition.

Where a validation is needed to follow up on that path and succeed to the next destination. But there were others who wanted a piece of the action. Out of nowhere they assumed they can come and go as they please, question a vision creating the wrong motivation.

Leaving you listing the faults and then them disguising them. Where the truth is not as important here what is imperative is you as an individual holding on to the final frontier. Letting things slide then preventing the corrupt from re-entering for their own safety was a challenge.

it left me harming my intuition. Creating an unbalanced vision, because I find myself in a position where I was preventing a positive energy from reinventing. There was no way I was going to feed off that presentation. For I was given an entrance all the way where it became a waste of energy.

Time subsided, because when everything fell into place, I could not let go or finalise another go. my passion is what gave me the power to feed off the vision. Trace it with the point of no return a view to consolidate while I finalising another clue, before you have a chance finalise another clue.

Where you end up fighting for your life, conditioning someone else hopes and dreams. Leaving you keeping up with the programme, so they can continue to have light while you are feeding off that insight. If you are not careful you will end up driving yourself incredibly insane.

Because you are in two minds, a cross road, a case that you must trace cancel close it. Facing your fears to get back on track feeding off that piece that gave you a chance to release. Erasing that pace would put me on a path of escaping another feast, where I had to release and find peace.

Before they had a chance to bring those challenges to fruition my method was being entertained by the head of that key that lead me to destination of giving me the wrong interpretation. A voyage that caved in on my intuition, that lead me to a destination where I had to get in.

Then advance my knowledge feed off the concept and win. It created a trap, to state a new fact to begin a new chapter one where the innocent mind that made me see it gave me the experience to feed off that greed. Where I stated the facts gave in to that method, and followed up on a trap.

Just to trick those who thought they could cloud my mind, by entertaining me with the notion they were tougher than I. Where I was pretending pending for an entrance that was positive and never ending. in fact, I was neglected, no longer depending on anyone.

Leaving the case to refine reform so when I got there, I was fully qualified. No turning back just looking inwards, while others were looking out, prying in my affairs hoping I would fail and set sail. Trying to get in by making me give in then hand them everything.

Where they were hitting me and running a definition of recognition. Just to hand them a position with revision. Spare me the melodrama, it is time I gave and granted them a taste of their own viewing. A poison, reviewing those conditions was based on a trace, handing me a test.

Just to cave in on the concept and erase that feast that was causing the wrong effects. Whatever was about to eventuate, it was creating a piece that was about to rejuvenate and release. Leading me to a destination revealing another hold up, a bold momentum that handed me clarification.

A chance to reveal a piece to that feast that was peaking. An awakening, to a presentation, leaving me exploring for a renewal. Instead of returning with denial, I decided to oust them all out. Reveal a trace, a trip down memory lane. A challenge to prevent them from ever return to torment me again.

CHAPTER 6

◆ ◆ ◆

TO LEAD THE CORRUPT TO DECEPTION TO FOLLOW UP ON ANOTHER REDEMPTION

Everything was finalised, even the parts that were entertaining. It was proving that my method was classed as correct. A way out on both ends, providing me with energy to clean cleanse then reveal a step towards the right direction. An ending to a debt that stalled, handing the nation restoration.

I no longer fail or fall just claim and cleanse. While I challenge, retrace a concept until the end. If I am not handed a chance to allow me to reverse, I will finally curse. A troubled method where the corrupt caused the fuss. With one awesome clue a challenge that cannot be refused or diffused.

That is to cancel them out so I can feed off that

poison and get through, that left me eyeing them because doubting myself anymore would lead me to a destination of cancelation. Where I had to retrieve it, all repeat another fall and if I am lucky, I get back up and rise above it all.

Where the repeat becomes a denial, to that play, a gamble to keep up with the programme. Where you get to see a challenge reveal itself, where repairing it will be imperial. For it will become a valid issue if you do not follow the right path, cave in on the concept and roam.

All by revealing how the corrupt like to state their vision. I got a chance to recall and recreate another disposition. Just to get in and calm those who tried to shaft me and then pretend nothing was done just so they can relate and steal another outcome.

Because some challenges are not worth perusing, returning to rekindle that flame. Will light up another fire to the game, a gamble where that presentation can reveal a lot about what the corrupt were planning next. That is to use others so they can continue to peak and feed off the method.

Just by creating the wrong piece. All so I can feed off the internal vision, with a proposition that caused the revelation. For my world to undo and create an intervention to clean up the mess and claim another feast to that treasure a gamble that gave me the power to release peace.

Where if you are not careful you can run the risk of losing that key, giving you the power to see. Many challenges come go and if you do not pick your fight and act quick you miss the beat. where the boat sailed you will be stuck failing another key, one where you to feed off the method.

A revelation to the corrupts deception. By holding them to contempt, where the piece was created before you had a chance to report and reveal the feast. Where that key that led you to that destination, was creating a validation to give those who conspire a challenge.

Where nothing is visible, nor clear unless you hit the frontier. Where if you are not careful the corrupt will, get away with harming you again. Because every time your vision caves in on the concept you will find yourself torn in two worlds, where you hit a hold up.

Where the only way to get back on track is stall. Poison those who try there hardest to harvest in your realm. For the position I was put in place before I had a chance to replace. Giving me the indication that my education was being tarnished and the only way I could varnish it.

Was feed off the concept and return and tarnish their method. Passing it with flying colours and not tracing it to give the corrupt a chance to reveal the man power in advance. For the method was refined it revealed a lot they all gave up. A time out to clear the debt, for it was each to their own.

There is no one powerful enough to fight me off. For those who could were not interested. There experienced, and experience individuals do not bother fighting back. because the entrance to unknown when you are fighting likeminded individuals is a waste of time there is no competition.

There is no need for it, for the end is a result is what gives you the power to align with spirit. While you get to live through it. Those who attack are demonic there not competitors nor leaders what they are, are fighters.

Individuals who are looking through the wrong rose-coloured glasses.

While I was on the move being considered by those Demon as high and mighty. It allowed me to enter the light the unknown, when they could not. Where I was handed the five heavenly Crowns. There was no completion for I was aligned with spirit, and others attached to me as if I was it.

The fact I was chosen to spread the message, did not make my life more visual or less hard. If anything, I suffered more, to get less forsaken for sure. A lesson well served, if you had a problem with me deal with it single heartedly. For you will not create an alliance to hold me to contempt.

Because there is no part missing the momentum will have you cantered. Dining with the devil to try to find gratification to that debt. For I was treated way too harsh, no one was giving me an opportunity the way it was meant to be, they were holding things back.

Handing me grief then return of my hardship. Where I lied to myself so I can keep with the program for that was the only way I could continue to create a feast to that piece. It was so off putting I could sense that once they completed their tasks, they would leave me stranded again.

Where reality would kick in. Where I would be back where I started. Holding on to a dream then repeating another scheme hoping for the best. While the corrupt progress was another position, I had to possess and create a war as I had them confess their debauchery, an immoral deception.

They were not to enter my domain, without my knowledge. For that thought pattern created a piece, a part you cannot release, until I trace trap and find peace. Dropping another bomb will create a feast, tormenting those who have the power to condition, contaminate devouring a fatal attempt.

Hitting that religious escapade, that went on to hit a siren. On the Assumption, the method will continue to keep strong. Exploiting those who had a clue with knowledge to devour those who were on the move, conceded. all while leading the innocent to a destination living a lie.

A life time of deception instead of resurrection. For they assumed the connection was unknown, and the trace was allowed to be roamed. The fact, it was acknowledged, do not phase them a bit. they were way to interesting to say the least, connecting to them before I had a chance to release.

Creating a beast, where I had to undo and follow up on a clue, then send the corrupt packing. On another venture, one where it will not eventuate it will only accommodate the rest will have to wait. Where they no longer have the power to create another redemption to my foundation.

For that second trail was a viable lesson, to hand me a condition to follow my path and every proposition. Time where the corrupt re-enter I can cut them out and lead them towards of a dead-end adventure. A new crew a clue that heaved at me and send me packing right through.

Where I will go back and forth, trying to release that demon that was holding me hostage. where it went viral cursing me at every mile, handing me denial. While I fed off that method case closed my perception changed it to the next confirmation where I witnessed, held up, on to a follow up.

So, when I hit my pinnacle, I can untrace, erase trap those who were pressuring me to push forward. For their own development assuming I was their final review. Considering I was there too, it did not make difference to them, where they could not wait to screw me right through.

All by silently connecting, click then when given half a chance disconnect. Relying on my spirit to light them up and leave me conditioned by one angle. That is to curse the corrupts method, while I reverse revealing another verse.

I came first and last to that test, it left me revealing a final request. Cornered me to release a piece, before my time while follow it through all by making me pay for a crime. To hand them the power to repeat hit me and run. Delete delay leaving me questioning my method all the way.

I had to uncover up another cover up, cave in on the concept. Then prevent them from ever returning to score a goal to challenge me to an entitlement I was owed. Instead of handing me my title, they all turned against me, fighting for a lost cause, turning my life in turmoil.

 Revealing an outcome, that gave me the power to condition another view. The one where I failed to condone, reform a revelation by feeding of that piece that handed me the restoration to uncover up another good deed. All while I was trying to create a better lead.

Just to get out of a world that was breeding hate instead of love. Leading me towards a dead-end destination, with no freedom to compare pretend and create a final leadership. Then reveal another kill and balance out that trace that had me feeding off the case with a final revelation to embrace.

Just to feed off the greed preventing the corrupt from ever re-entering. Where it led me to a destination of a story untold, before I was caved in on, lead to believe something else, while I was being sold and auctioned out to the cheapest buyer.

All while they were scheming to scar me again, lining me up for another dead end, for I was on the mission to cleanse my spirit, from one end to the next, keeping balanced was another conquest. For their vision was a curse where the concept was leaving me holding onto another final degree.

It was feeding me a whole lot of Malarkey. Where the idea became a vision added with a vampire effect, a challenge I could not manage or change to save myself from that defect. Unless I personally attacked those who were conspiring to attack me it got to the point, I had to finalise a feast.

Just get back on track and release peace. On the condition I never have to rely on those who assume they can hit me and run and get by on another hold up. An outcome that gave me the power to solve that position added with the experience to follow up on disposition.

I decided the next best thing was to let it go, create a piece that gave me passion to find peace. Make sure when I return, I do not need to gamble a thing, I had retrained my mind to accept everything. Even the parts that lined me up for disappointment, just to overcome another curse.

As I declare decline, deepen my soul, and challenge that trace. Give into that personal vendetta to make my life better. Erase another feast to that piece a condition it so I cannot release all because I was being fed off by an entertainer who had entrance.

Where that method was conditioned by a stab in the back and the wound was healed by yours truly. This time around that system that was created in my piece are nowhere to be found. because I am way too profound. That key now is safe and sound with me, holding on to a second rounder.

A foundation that hands me accreditation to give me the power to create a piece. While I follow up on another distinction, creating the resolution where I need to cave in on the concept and succeed. My mind was in two wave lengths, conquer face my fears and not let anyone get me down.

The other was to learn to live within me on means, lean towards my own beliefs and accept defeat. Whenever things did not turn out the way it was meant to and be so hard on myself, because in the end that freedom was my friend it gave me a chance to free myself from past intervals.

It left me researching for answers that never eventuated. While wasting valuable time going back and forth for a vendetta, because in the end all it does is hold your contempt where if you look forward you run the risk of hitting a dead end.

For those who created a piece to win me over, no longer have the power to release. For the assumption of entering my realm and heaving at me over again is no longer in mist. For I had a long way to go, more to see, what it would be like to be me with more knowledge.

Because others like to enter my realm, renown in my centre. Then attempt to build a foundation around it then try there hardest to accomplish another harvest. A feast to create a powerful piece one that will finalise the outcome I need to find a meaning for that imperial momentum.

Just to hand me an outcome that will hand me the piece, feed off the concept and release. Translating it, in a way where my method will not lead me astray. For those who conditioned it to rely on me for repetition will have to pay me in recission.

Or else they will run the risk of reliving a nightmare. One where they cannot return and stare at me in the face assuming we are in on this race together, competing with one another to see who is stronger. In the end, I out did them, then out did myself by dreaming instead of making it happen.

Relying on presentation that handed me the constant reminder I was heading towards a compensation. I was meant to be funded, where I am owed a substantial amount of money but I went for mind body and spirit instead I found that pays out any debt.

Because no one lives for ever, so why not feed of the endeavour by devouring the honour. The only way to state it was to create a piece and state without warning those who were part of it to get out and start fresh because my lead was a destination where I could return later.

Then breath out another personal feast. Where I can back on track and release a piece that gave me a chance to see I was on the right path, a clean way out. Where I can look back and remind myself, I am right on track now. The foundation was to create the restoration to hand me social preservation.

A restitution from that restriction, so conceal another competition. However, the plan backfired for the corrupt played a dirty trick and wanted to cover up another debt. All by handing me death threats added by dead ends. The anxiety and fear took over as I found myself repeating a fight.

The only way to repeat, and not compete was not live in fear and delete. Without delaying a meeting, this time was walk face my fear from within. A recondition to revise pressure the corrupt handing me that key that was owed to me. In mind body and spirit added with a touch of dignity.

An entitlement to create a piece and follow up on another feast, where they were to present me with an entitlement, denying me access will be a final review, that will give me the power to screw them right through. Where I no longer have failure to my amendments.

I went through the whole nine yards, trapping those who conditioned it right through. Make sure when I hit the end twice, I bounce right back up no longer a must, just sacrifice, and create another device. I was on a mission second third fourth time around creating competition.

It handed me a position that was meant to face me with repetition. For acknowledging my accomplishments was one key waiting for me to clear the path was another. Where I paused, then caused an effect created a piece went back on track and released a condition to find peace.

A revelation to that destination, that will clear my path cleanse my spirit and lift me right up to the next position. One where I have repetition reconditioning my vision where I had to validate another point of view to get back on track and propose another key where I meet the corrupt half way.

Reveal a case, where the corrupt were not waste that prediction on a case that was forthcoming. here everyone knew the ending for it was prewritten, for it never came to fruition. It led me to another destination where I missed out and someone else took over half of my presentation.

Where the other half is still pending, for all I felt was pressure to that resurrection. where truly I should have felt pleasure reaching the next destination. Others wanted a piece of the action handing me a whole lot of drama a trace where I lost my train of thought.

Where the only way, I could get back on track was find a place I can sit back relax and feel safe. Where that method took a decade to relay messages and prove my prediction, a revision to state another contradiction a pleasure added with conviction.

Where I get to lead preach and put the corrupt in a position, a destination with no foundation just hands them that presentation that will give me the reservation to keep up with the programme. I was idling, waiting for the right moment to save myself from that hold up.

A bold role up, that kept me suffering, from within, while the corrupt were mastering another plan. Just to get me to give in have me sacrifice my soul so they can win everything. Stabbing me in the back accusing me of things that were supposedly to come true, created a rumour.

It caved in on me. and I was failing every attention to detail. Making up stories of how I will turn out in the end I hit a nasty gamble on their end, where they took that risk and it paid off with dividend on both ends. But little did they know I had recission, revision and a vendetta on my end.

From what was achieved in the past was a nasty karmic reaction. A follow up to the next destination. Set in stone side by side back on track traced and trapped. Where those who were in on it will need to build a new foundation around me, repeating a new key.

Where this time around I caused an effect created a

challenge. Then starved the corrupt of repetition and revision. Where they had no choice but to hand me what they owe me with no condition no repetition and no second time to return to repeat and delve into another crime.

I was given a fighting chance to rejoice follow it through no questions asked no added clue. whatever I had done in the past, was to be forgotten and forgiven. For what I experienced to reach my potential was even worse an absolute curse I could not reverse a challenge that failed me.

They were meant to grade me with high extinction a pass towards a development where my strengths and intuition were to come to fruition. For I was meant to come first preach my views and continue to climb the ladder hitting another final matter.

It was a fact, if we are to replay, they were to allow me to enter and save me and continue to do so. For they need me more than I needed them. Where they went to such extremes to harm me again because I did not give in. Where I was going through that tribulation and rapture from within again.

I had to go through it twice for I was caved on before I had a chance to reveal a key in advance. Personally attacked by those who were not strong enough and assumed latching on to me by feeding me was another part of their malarkey.

Giving them another chance to cover up a sin in advance. Where I had carried that burden all on my own, reminding my soul it will be over and I will get to live life one day at a time. Silently releasing another condition where I can enjoy that pain with recognition.

Where I spat out venom blood and semen from my scrotum just to find that condition that handed me repletion added with repetition. Why would I share victory with those who do not deserve or desire to return and help me, when I need it too,

For what I had to offer was part of a treaty dignified and give me the energy I needed to repeat and feel alarmed because the corrupt were questionable lining me up for a desire to hit back and finalise that case that served me well in the end of the race. Reserving me the right for an established event.

One where I cave in on the spirit and create a repetition, to clean out that mission. It led me to destination of death threats and dead ends. Listing the faults of those who return to contaminate my soul, in a world where that method no longer holds me to contempt.

CHAPTER 7

◆ ◆ ◆

WHEN THE WORLD CREATES AN EFFECT, A CHANCE TO RESSERECT.

Waiting for the next conquest, the freedom,
was a revelation to the next destination. Not in
true faith nor face value. For no one ever faces
you unless they have an ultimatum. Creating
a clue to hand you a destination with a final
classification a reminder to end that reservation.

Where the room with a view, become an entrance towards another dimension. For there was no value to those who were two faced, it was just a preparation to undo a feast and reserve that presentation to hand out another beast, a mission that caves in on the system.

I get to relay messages to undo a part, where the corrupt assume they have the power to consume. Kicking up another fuss as they resume. Feeding off the concept while

61

I kept pretending, for what I was expecting was more than I was envisioning not only I saw the light but the over view was a fight.

Where they assumed they knew it all, in fact they knew nothing. For my presence was their trace to continue to create a piece to keep me from losing my place. For I was working towards creating a challenge that went too far and beyond what I knew and that was to take control of another cue.

The only way I could reveal that revivification was to fight back and survive. All by making sure I keep up with the program and stay stagnant no more. Live and let learn, holding on to one more clue, making sure I use it wisely. So, when I reach my pinnacle no one will have power to divide me.

Returning for a chance to rebirth, was delay based on that method that served me well in the end of that play. A dilemma that hit me when I hit that final tremor, For I hit a guessing game and my method was way to advance to overcome an outcome.

This time around I added symmetry to the game, a method that cannot push me away. Because I relived a drama, that was overdue, that been said with all due respect no one has the power to mate or meet me half way because I got over it long ago where I fell into a dead heat in the end.

I was confronted with a conviction. Convinced me of the power that followed through. In the end it was a dirty trick for the corrupt to skip that too. Whether I come out pretending, it was enough for me to witness I closed one door and opened another, where the other side was creating a piece.

It served me well warned me I was about to get through hell, I was abandoned. Handed energy to delete delay and have my dream become a reality. A backup where I get to see that feature fast forward, a debt paid out in full. No report just a fact a reaction, handing me power for deception.

Whether the method worked in my favour is a story about to unfold. I had to come back with a vengeance to prove my point; For my innocence was being tarnished, while the corrupt were using me to varnish that clue. Repeating another day to skip, scam a point, revealing the corrupts trace.

Then live through that method after denying me access in a world I created through peace. Where the only way I could perform that act of kindness. A preventative measure that served me well at every treasure the corrupt from returning and undoing another yearning.

I was on needed to complete a task and undo a clue. Reserving the right to force my way in, finalising a decade of whatever was holding me back. Creating a challenge to get me on track. A placement that handed me a point of no return a review to cheapen the deal.

Then skip the corrupt right through, restoring the energy that had me repeating another trial. A trace to hand me denial and a vision that was serving me at every competition. I did everything I could to enlarge that cause and effect serving me a sentence all by reserving the right a vengeance.

Where others like to return stir the pot, throw a little venom here and there. Then assume they have the upper hand to come and go as they please. Reminding me of a past event that had me fighting for my life, while the rest were living there's.

Several had a plan but not one knew how it will end, for it was me in the end that will finish first and come last. All while the rest will have to wait for me to undo the mess. For what they created accumulating all that unwanted debt. A feast towards a free ride an ending that was pending.

While I handed the corrupt an added key to that challenge, a chance to plot for revenge. A case not worth restarting or reliving, for the method was a dead end. I might as well give in and save myself from another failed attempt, to make sure my precious stone will not wither or fail me again.

For this time around I failed nothing, it was an attempt to earn a key. A chance to free my head from a made-up story that led me to a destination of creating a personal vendetta. Where I was repeating started a foundation of my own, given an opportunity see the outcome that suited me well.

Where the rest will have to play it in a way where I cave in on the system. Lead them to a destination where they no longer have revision, just a follow up where I have returned to clear the debt. Make it clear what they owe me will create a feast to bring them pain in mind body and soul.

Just so I can continue to take control of my own proposition. Call it the power of suggestion, not only did they give me the upper hand to save myself from that apprehensive vision. It led me to a destination, where this time around my reputation is what it is.

I might use it to my advantage and milk if for what it is worth. Hit run and call it an outcome that will favour me in the long run a presentation with a foundation to hand the corrupt recission. Where the rest will cave in on the concept and hand me repetition a competition to feed off the conclusion.

Just so, I can get that increase the one that I need to succeed, revealing another hit and run as I proceed. However, it was stated and recreated it was worth more than the thought itself. For I was less than what they imagined, more than I could sense by returning to retrieve, a waste of time

For they were way out of line. They all went too far and so did I, for the difference between them and I, was I had a momentum to create a temperance. Added with a temperament, between me the Gods and the Holy spirit that was holding me hostage.

Turning my head upside down, was a method, that created a piece. Before I had a chance to state it, the drama took its toll, and the corrupt took control of me and my spirit. Stuck in a deliverance. It gave me the passion to proceed, no more fighting a lost cause, where I was given a reason to breed.

For the presentation was a validation to hand me a key, just so I can hit that next destination. Without holding on to a shocking revelation. Looking back validate that trap, skipped those who were tracking me down and feeding off my method while not making a sound.

Where I was overlooking a past event, back tracking would become unnecessary. For feeding off that violation would give me the presentation to motivate and then escape from that dead end. An entrance, I no longer wish to pretend nor protect those who do not deserve to be in it.

Because they entered under false pretences, the game was ending. It became an expenditure where the corrupt will not have enough medallions to afford to erupt. Or even the condition that sentence that served me prior to reserving the right to premeditate that fight.

It handed me a vengeance that returned and prevented me from reliving a pause an effect. For that never ending story will result for them surrendering, for I fell into a deep sleep. A curse I could not reverse, unless I handed them a verse, just for me to come first.

Handing them the power to trace trap counteract a fake and final fact. A contract where I reach that trace and they breach it assuming they will get away with causing the effect and hitting me and running the risk of deserting leaving me silently suffering, while the rest recreate another conquest.

For that trace handed the corrupt a chance to encourage me to release, one more final piece. A review hitting them at every final, a time out to sweeten the deal. Then prevent them from releasing a vision to that competition a dead end to that presentation that gave me the power to pretend.

For a feast that could not entertain me was reserving me the right to violate and frame he who likes to return with on more turn. Assuming he has the power to turn tricks, but in fact all he had was a dead end to release that final piece that served me well at the end of that lease.

Because the recognition had arisen way before the game became forbidden. The concept had come to an end, they could not afford to get out or continue. For that free ride they once had was a trick, a trap, a craving to get back on track with, an empty case full of promises.

So, when I hit my pinnacle, I could shut that case completely. Neither look back or forward or be strung along any longer. No longer stuck in the middle of dilemma a delay or a tremor, for I was causing an effortless effect, listing the faults of those who tried to use me to resurrect.

For the game was a gamble a gift handed to me on the condition I meet those standards. While I keep up with the programme. Repeating a bad day was going to push me further into a demeaning dilemma. A key I could not free myself from, a challenge I had to repeat report and cause an effect.

So, I never lose my status, for I was forced and the only way in caused an effect a version of that A revision I could not change because that presentation was way to out of line. For those who knew, wanted to get in so desperately could not wait to face me attack my spirit.

All by giving me the indication I was heading towards the wrong destination. The fact they had me cornered was enough for me to see I was winning periodically. So, I decided to retrace follow my instincts. Close that case return later and revive another dead end.

Just so I can get back on track and pretend. Where I could not wait to finalise, by trying to survive another cold case a clean way out so I don't lose my place. Where the characteristics to that foundation made my energy somewhat causing the effects.

A need to feed off that sacrament, that handed me the feast to rely on the piece that gave me the passion to release and find peace. Where That presentation was a dedication, that lead me to wrong destination. A decision to challenge me in a fight, competing with me on every occasion.

The only way they could see beyond the now, was prevent me from reliving my destiny. Lucky for me that was a joke too, I was handed a chance to return evoke. Prevent the corrupt from returning for a yearning. For in the end, they needed me and my permission to grant a new mission.

Where I get to hit the next scene. Finalise the drama in-between, where I was lucky again. I was idling, looking for ways to save my soul sweeten the load and create a better abode. For I was not giving in, I was taking a chanced in advanced to relive another fascist momentum.

Where I was just relaying messages. For those who were creating the piece were stealing my thunder so they can release. During the process they were feeding others too and for those who were on the move were feeding. Handed a wish or two, just so they can screw me right through.

It got to the point I caved in on the concept, mellowed with the vision a provision based on the situation that took away the confusion that landed me the part that I needed to find peace. It gave me the power to chase away those demons in my head.

Because they were cheating on me to get ahead. For there were to many of them following me right through, turned against me cursing my existence competing with my soul instead of giving me back what was owed to me. I was Gambling all of it way, so I do not lose my third eye along the way.

I had to hold back to get back on track. Reminding myself that my trace was case that gave me the power to set back another pace one where I can trace and erase that pre warning that handed me the scandal. Just to get back on track follow up on a condition one where I can repeat another vision.

Little did I know at the time I would lose my mind trying to state a final review. Where a decade past. Realizing I did not miss a task or fail a feast, I was just passing through. Reliving a drama where the obstacle became no longer critical to that analysis just a diversion to hand me poison.

The one that created the confusion. I just past another mission a reminder to the next proposition to get through, where hell will break loose if the corrupt don't hand me that final review. So, I can follow up a get in winning all while poisoning the corrupts method right through.

Where the presentation to the corrupts restoration had become a final revelation. Handing me the cancelation key to move forward. It handed me validation to give the unjust a chance to sweeten my soul in advance. Added with deception ammunition a condition that they kept repeating.

Where they were no longer sweeping it under the carpet. As they were proceeding, returning the favour was part of the saviour. It got to the point I no longer wanted to fight back so I fixed it purely to get back on track. Traced it so when they return, so they cannot scheme or repeat.

I caught them in the act of revealing another theme. That proposition I was feeding off, had given me a portion of that extortion back to the sender. Where in the back of my mind was trying to find a balance to create a silence. For my thoughts were running wild and I knew I was hitting a damn case.

Where I can open and shut another feast to that piece. Where I leave the corrupt entertained with the notion, they had predictions but in fact what they have is a resolution that will restore their reservation, handing me a cancelation key to continue my path.

I no longer feeding off those conditions. Because it was a contradiction not a prediction that made me scheme a reality to that theme. Where I became resilient to the impression, that was giving me the depression hounded by the key that gave me the vision to see beyond the now.

Where I saw I was about to hit bad news and the only way out was to trace trap get my keys and counteract. I was falling into a trap a competition added with composition stalling long enough to wrap the corrupt in a web of lies one where they cannot stand to be around one another.

Where they become paranoid. For I was on the wrong path being mistreated and trapped in a world where no one wanted to know me. but when they needed me, they handed me a clue. It landed right t where they planted me and then let me down nice and easy.

How friendly they were trying there hardest to cover up another casualty. Because they kept losing every time, where they had a chance to revive and reveal another crime. Hoping if I make a mistake they can return and harm me holding on to the next talent.

Hoping I will fall, fail not rise above it all and some other vampire takes over my role, leaving me absolutely hollow. Where did they get off heaving at me all the way, God knows! All I knew I faced my fears got through to the next dimension, carried a burden long enough to finalise another clue.

I can reveal the truth, keep up with the program and make sure I do not lose hope and become a recluse. When I hit the next duration that destination will free me from reservation. Where they were trying my hardest not to lose myself, the soul that got me through, created a spurt of energy.

Just to keep me balanced, hammering me in the head just so I can look ahead. Not fall into a trap of failure and death threat ends, for my foundation collapsed, I had to do was rebuild another path one that created the piece that gave me the power to chase away the blues a chance to release peace.

Reserving that case that gave me the extra power to cave in on the method, followed by a sense of relief, a scent of a woman a flower that grew in the mist of all who knew. Where it created a lie to help the corrupt get by. While they continue to feast face follow up on a free ride to the other side.

A point of view where I got a chance to erase and relay a message or two to those who knew and wanted to clean up that mess so I can cancel it all out. Handing them clues so I round it up and mess up my head to give them another chance to get ahead.

What a foundation I had to conceal just to pull through another follow up on a point of view, that gave the power to resume. not give up or give in. Because I had too much to live for and my passion was my window to opportunity, where I had to keep fighting for my life to get there.

Not repeat another follow up. Where I had to return the favour and uncover up a dilemma that the corrupt created through peace a terrible lie that handed me the failure and then the power to get by. All by assuming, I was their final revelation, constantly on my raider abusing me like no other.

Hounding me in the head to hand them a key or have me suffer in silence until I get there. What a difference a day made when I was carrying a burden silently revolving as the corrupt were driving me towards a dead-end destiny. Onto the next feed, a contest added with a quest.

Just to pretend to track down feed off another trend. Where I had no time to feast or hand the corrupt another piece. For I released a passage way, where I had to stay alert carry on to the next position one where I had repetition. Leading me to a destination that stated the facts.

Carried onto the next foundation a piece that repeated another cause an effect that made me see I was on to a huge reservation restoring a distinction. Between those who knew and those who like to share with those who don't have a clue. Going back and forth was the only way I could cash in.

Then resolve another win, preventing the corrupt from re-entering again. Trying my hardest to release a piece, a condition based on an assumption. Just to give me the power to recreate another vision, an audition that went wrong creating a vindictive interlude.

To catch the corrupt before they fed off my energy, became another cosmetic challenge. Where I had to enter the industry and try my hardest to prove I was the chosen. Little did I know I had competitors to trap me and try they hardest to see if they can ravel my destiny.

Put in competitive position where I lost my light, my vision to cave in on the concept. Pray for a composition. Then face my fears pray for another day to replay, releasing that contamination that was planted in my soul. A condition I had to relinquish to connect to that bleak leak.

It was leaving me terribly oblique. Where I was relying on the lustre to that piece, not the part that handed me the creativity to return for a key. A part that was holding me back, I had to fast forward feed off the method that created a challenge handed me the energy I needed to get back on track.

I was being traced trapped, tricked pushed in the corner sealed with a kiss from another dimension. Where my creativity was being torn and the only way, I was going to revive a feast was return the favour and release. Holding on to a key one where I please myself as I continue to flourish.

Relying on those who faced me, assuming they have the power to fail me. Silently revealing another bad feeling, cancelling out another revision to that feast that had me providing the corrupt with the honour to continue to dishonour. A method where I had to endure, cave in on the concept and stall.

Then stay strong long enough so the corrupt do not steal my thunder once more. I was planting a key of my own a seed where others were trying there hardest to receive. A condition to attempt to contradict a mission, by creating a repetition that will give me the permission to lash out.

It was posing a threat on those who were competing assuming to compare and try to compel will become amusing. It was sacrificing my spirit and putting me through hell. A follow up to the next meet, a condition I could not retrace, erase, or feed off unless I repeat.

Where I had to get back on track, start another fight, then rely on my instincts to get me by. Who had time for that punishment, it was way too harsh to recreate another damn bad day. For I had to many enemies and I did not want to put myself through that pain again!

CHAPTER 8

◆ ◆ ◆

THE TURN OF EVENTS THAT CREATED THE MISSING LINK TO THAT KEY THAT MADE ME SEE "BEYOND REGONITION."

All while causing effects and giving into that proposition. I could see a feast developing, where I was warned that others were attempting another shame to my name. Just to finalise that love and hate relationship. It was causing the wrong effects a steep level of miscommunication.

It left me questioning everything, even the parts that gave me an indication. Confirming the obvious, I was hitting a stream of events some worse than others. Where I became aware and vigilant to that final request. Leading me to a destination creating a piece that will hand me release.

A reservation to deceit, and follow up on another meet. It became overbearing, carrying a burden where now every time I play, I fall into the trap of being afraid to mate, or doing anything pleasurable. Because my expectations did not meet with my desires and disappointment took over.

The only way, I could undo was create a piece revaluate my situation and find peace. Because I realized in the mist of it all the whole situation was a clue to hand me that fluke. Just so I can continue to create a piece and follow up on another feast.

I gave in and caved in on the concept and played it purely to get back on track, evaluate and not look back. Focus on something worthwhile, live my life to the fullest. For whatever energy I had left I had created the freedom I need to progress, only to rely on no one thing conceal another theme.

One where I can get back on track and follow up on another final scheme. A deception to validate the corrupts scheme of themes. I took that freedom for granted, where it gave me the power and passion to pass another disposition with discretion.

Where I no longer wish to live in denial because I was rejecting my identity. Not allowing myself to blossom, for I had the belief that everything I stated eventually will get rejected anyway. Little did I know, I was being torn, pushed in the corner, shoved in two worlds and both were nasty.

I could sense hostility; it was creating a war in my peace teaching me lessons. Where I was falling and been falsely accused abused and left to suffer. Where I could not fail or enlist in another trace because I hit a piece that led me to a path I could not let go of.

I had to follow my path and prevent the corrupt from returning. I was left pretending that their life was pending because my mission and story was never ending. For each time I served that individual who had been through it all. It played in the back of my mind that was I being used again.

What a surprise! With nowhere else to turn and nothing to fall back on. I found myself hitting a never-ending battle. While I rose above all odds fell and risen above the rest, envisioning a new me a test. Where I must confess it gave me the energy I needed to compress.

I kept following my route to keep to myself from failing. While I was living and breathing that entity, that was handing me the feast. I was handed a piece I needed to release; I was given a second chance in advance to praise those who assumed I was there to bring them luck.

In fact, I was reaching my vision and handing them a dead end, one where my freedom to pretend is no longer on the mission. For I could play it any which way I liked, reach my peak face my fears repeat a challenge look forward not back and remind myself no more doubt or denial, back on track.

Placing everything I learnt in order, was a challenge I had to go back in time recreate another final foundation to store my energy and feed off the synergy. So, when I hit that last and final key I could let go and no longer pretend, because it was nothing but a no show.

I played the game relied, on no body to keep my train of thought balanced. To continue to develop my talents. For those messages I needed to feed off were lies and those who were greedy were serving me with a challenge blind sighting the whole concept.

All I wanted to do was recreate a fluke, so I can go back in time and revaluate that fleet. For it was reflection time it brought me to my knees. What more could I ask for and what more could I do to create an investigation, for the instigation took me for a fool and was interrogating me.

I was in a trance a chance to see how far they would take it. Closing one door and opening another, was the next final step to the next destination. It was an open and shut case an easy to install, recall and face whatever come to fruition. where that piece was resembling a challenge.

It took me for a fool and left me repeating another meeting. Just so I can release, just to prove I that I was being stalked. Pushed in the corner so the corrupt can redevelop and make up more stories in my head so they can get ahead. Recreating a challenge so I can get ahead

Wanted more of what they could handle, an extension to that warranty. I assuming I was there and all I needed was guidance handed me the trace and the chance to follow up on another trance. Return for a scandal in advance. A day did not go by where I did not feel welcome.

I felt that I was being torn in a world, where I was not wanted. Just needed for a short amount of time, once they achieved their goal, they cut me off. It was enough to follow up on a journey that had me reserving the right to accommodate a challenge repeating another trial.

A method that handed me denial, but broadened my horizons. It brought me in and handed me a chance to cheat on all of those who assumed using me will bring them good news. while being brought forward on the intention I get fed off, a joke that was about to provoke a case to go.

Handing the corrupt another admission, admiring their presentation was a confirmation that led me to a destination where I had to report them. I had no choice for they were causing effects, feeding off that presentation releasing a debt and heaving at the concept.

It was enough for me to face a degree, of challenges, if I was to pass it. It would give the corrupt a piece of their own filth a lesson well earned on my end on their end it will be a regret until the end. trapping those who encourage me to eradicate will give me the power embrace it.

It was another key all I needed was a chance to advance to trace that one thought. For it served me well in the end of the race, just so I can get through and not look back and review another trap. Having the audacity to recreate another feast on my destiny was a varsity of thoughts.

I was gathering my thoughts and creating a conclusion, for I was not a neglecting a thing on my end. I had to many obstacles' fake friends and no freedom to pretend. Leaning towards an effect, just to torment and haunt those who consider themselves as revolutionist.

Where I had to do Shut that one door that was holding me back and open a new one. Was a better conclusion to my journey back-to-back. One where I can get back on track release a piece feed off that mark that handed me the muck, a mind reading game that made no sense to me.

It ended up becoming a gamble in the end. A messy situation where I was constantly on the mark, spot on, ready and willing to claim another nark. An intense singular momentum to create a state of mind. Space out those who subside coincide and continue to divide and conquer on my side.

With that energy that caved in on me, it saved me and served me well added with an interlude. All while trying to intrude with another improvement to that emotional roller coaster. The one that stated the facts and created the wrong faith.

While covering up another cancelation key, where I was about to lose my dignity. For it fell in the hands of, he who had it in for me. Where if I continue my path, I can reclaim another drive, an interaction with those who were in on it, changing the perception of those who condition.

Just by creating another restoration, to that violation. Return with redemption, challenging my thoughts all while fighting off those demons and revealing another feast that took me by surprise and chased me in disguise.

Creating a sacrament, where I had to sacrifice follow up on another fight. Leading me towards a path that had me revealing my truth, unravelling another knot to my stomach to hand the corrupt a chance to revive my spirit so I can survive another revision. A temperament with supervision.

Creating an interlude, a resilience to that mission to make way for a day. Where I can return and press replay. So, when I hit that last and final recall, I could return the favour and solemnly swear that the mission was on looking, working towards my direction, revealing another contradiction.

A prediction added with a reminder of a past event, that was handing me a feast to that piece. Where I was constantly trying to figure out what I did wrong, how I can get out of that mess and what to do to get the corrupt to confess.

Because it was leaving me feeding off the mission, handing the corrupt competition. Instead of creating a piece, to hand me admission, there was a repeat. For the corrupt will intentionally make an error to have me return and surrender. I was always on the run, trying to release that final.

Find some sort peace, balance in between fear and faith. Where I was failing at every cause an effect because I lost that fortitude that I needed to cancel out that trend. Where I caved in on the mission without losing competition. Using methods to cave in on the concept.

Just release negativity towards my direction, waiting for me to fail so they can resume connect and to enter another dimension. Creating an intervention an interaction that gave me the energy to fail every redemption, continue my path feast off those who assume they were generating energy.

In fact, they were feeding off me, it caved in on me, powering through just to consume. Then follow up on another route. For they assumed they were demonic, where they had super natural powers, could control the universe, by using those who had vision and interpreting it as their own intuition.

It was preventing others from creating a piece to. It will be disturbing the peace, of those who were causing the effects. Leaving everyone who was part of it in Desiree right through. God, forbid they get challenged too, where others get a chance to bid, for their method was way out of line.

A cold-hearted effect it created a bad mood. Swinging from one end to the next, where every chance I had gave me the indication I was reserved for another allegation. Where they were stalking me at every challenge trapping me in the corner summoning me to.

Just so they can cash in and validate another final review. Just to cause an effect and present me with a clue. While burning me right through, trying to see what they could do to blind sight me. Challenge me with integrity and take away my power and take control.

A method that was stolen from me long ago. It became a dead end with a death threat a trail of negative thought patterns where I was stuck living a lie to hand the corrupt another chance to get by. An error of judgement, from my end was a clue, for I had to contemplate another restoration.

My foundation was about to collapse. At that crucial momentum, that is when I knew I hit an ending that was pending. A redemption that had me repeating another final meeting. Where I end up losing faith create caution to the wind and lead myself to destination where end up losing track of time.

Everything I worked for to keep in line, will slither through my fingers. I will end up losing again interrogated for a crime the corrupt commit. Just to frame me, what a lie to get the truth. Looking back at it all, that momentum was nothing but a state of mind creating a sense of reality.

Where I had to try my luck, follow up on a path clearing another bad day. Before it became a challenge, where I would follow my route. Hand the corrupt a chance to follow me in advance and cut me up so they can continue to trace trap and trick me again.

I had to condition another conspiracy, so when I hit my pinnacle, I could state a new fact create an optical illusion and get back on track. Make sure the corrupt never have the power to control my destiny. The plan backfired for the thought they knew was a challenge that got me through.

Where I can create a piece change my destination any which way I please and create a definitive attribute that stated a fact got me through and lead me to a destination that made me feed off the concept instead of living it. I was tricked trapped traced and conned into thinking otherwise.

Meanwhile, those who were in on it were saving themselves and handing me a second trial. A dead end added with denial. Now that I am here I could not careless I lived that dream that ended up become a nightmare because others who were in on it were conspiring to bring me down.

All by giving into me. Then when my hopes hit a high note I went down with it, on the condition I never fail another repetition, so when I hit my pinnacle, I no longer deny myself truth trace and the bedevilment to repeat another case.

While they were trying there hardest to scheme, return the favour by lining me up for another hit and run, where the outcome lessoned and I fell into another trap and the only way out was to relapse. Coming out of that thought wave, was giving me a conscious awareness.

It gave me the impression I was out on my own creating a peace. Trying my best not to allow that test to fail me. Before I had a chance to relive it, feed off the trance. I was on the brink of losing my mind, for I went way to far, fantasizing of what life would be like if I had that dream come true.

Little did I know I was dreaming to much about what I was about to achieve. I lost track of time; my mind went with the trace missing the boat. I was creating a drama ahead of time, so when I reached my pinnacle, I was out of line, realized the path I was put on was purely to hand that key to another.

Just so they can further while I lose my faith and the intention that followed. Leaving me disguising the truth following the intention so I never reach my potential and the corrupt keep feeding off it. I was not organised, and everything started to fall out of place.

I lost control my mind trying to find my place in a world where I was replaced. Just to get ahead I had to repeat retrace erase and follow up on a pace. A free ride to the other side, cave in on the concept and subdivide. Leading the corrupt to a destination where that freedom was causing a tremor.

What they once knew was cut short, where the only way to repeat was to report, torment those who knew, while supporting me right through. For they assumed I had no worth and cheating on me will trace repeat and encourage me to return for another yearning.

A method to challenge a chase to trace that case that served me well and prepared me for hell. Where I was given the will power and the strength to get through and reveal another clue. Because he who latched onto me was also feeding off me.

My ideas were challenged with the notion I was not in, but in fact I was being pushed off the edge so I never get in. My concept changed, it left me silently forming an energy that created the wrong piece, lying to myself was the only way I could find and release peace.

Returning the favour was a challenge I could not proclaim, I was being shocked by the system, torn, and trapped in a world where the corrupt were about to harm me in my domain. No one was facing me, the way they were meant to, creating a war in my peace.

I had to go through, fighting it off, was way worse for wear. I swore I will never put myself through that unworthy again. I was scared out of my whits, I hit whits end a never-ending story where I got a chance to refine and follow up on another cause, that made no sense.

An effect that took its toll and distanced me from the rest. A chase I could not reveal unless I took a challenge and fed off that presentation, to that destination that gave me the power to hand in my resignation. A case I could open naturally, close whenever necessary.

Accompanying the notion I can compress my energy, when needed periodically. All so I do not waste time using it, feed off the conceded for those who assumed they had power to revolve, made me see I had a challenge to create a feast to that piece.

That method was pulling me forward, it held me back. Where the only way to get back on track was consume the energy that was feeding off me. I had left the end of that key to a position serving the corrupt a case they could not erase, chasing butterflies to get back on track.

All while starving myself of attention, so I can continue to feast of the redemption, violating another competition. Giving the corrupt a chance to case close, and hand me a that key. The one they owed me. About to hit a cheap shot of my own a cancelation key to feed off the transition of the mission.

Keeping up with the program was handing me a dependency. A method that was serving the corrupt. Where I had to unravel it all, then present the corrupt with a violation to their arrangement. Challenging my path so I can find peace and then when the time come overcome a nasty outcome.

Interrogated me with an instigation, to replace me with a final revelation, restoring my energy. Holding me hostage so they can return later to compete with me, was a thing of the past. For there was no competition here. It was a message, a nasty thought that caved in on me.

Where my presentation remained vigilant in the back on my mind. Just to get back on track, make it happen create a feast to say the least. I gave in, I had no choice and the conditions were helping me rejoice. Meeting me all the way was a method undone, handed a better outcome.

Little did I know at the time I was to return and repeat another crime, restoring my energy. while I was getting refining another clue. Close one door and open another and make sure before I do, I uncover another debt. one where the corrupt are about to get a taste of their own karmic residue.

Time to undo repent and skip those who knew, for it was long overdue. For all I knew I was put on a path where I failed to return for, he who knew prior did not want to be part of my world nor allow me to enter pick up where I left off learn a lesson then cut them off.

Where I decided to work against those who knew. Feeding off my veracity that linger in the corrupts society. I was vague, beginning a new task at the time was huge, and difficult. My negativity was overriding the whole concept, my vanity took over; I had no idea how to calm my thoughts.

My head that was spacing me out I could not see ahead.

Leading me towards a destination, creating so much doubt in my mind I had no time out. I was too busy trying to break free from all those dead ends added with death threats. I had certain individuals wanting to teach me a lesson.

In the end, I decided to give in, allow them to follow me from within, I had no choice. I was pushed off the edge and no one was favouring me. Every time I hit an outcome a dead end will follow, presented with a challenge where I was jinxed and the only way to repeat it was become a minx.

CHAPTER 9

◆ ◆ ◆

COMMUNICATING WITH MY INNER SELF TO RESTORE THE ENERGY THAT CAVED IN ON ME

---

*I felt I had to learn a lesson to create a piece,
harm those who put fuel to the fire. Assume
they have power to create a war in my peace.
All so they can return at a later date retrieve,
perceive and follow up on another deed. In
the end their method was a dead end.*

The contract we had was breached, they did not go through with the plan. They made me play the game on the condition they save me along the way. In fact, all it did was interpret that view and hand me a point of view a presentation to refine the next destination.

I stayed alert, on the feast to release so I can find peace. Left suffering in a world where I felt unsafe troubled at every formation, terribly following the wrong path to salvation. I started listening to my head instead of my heart for my instincts were kicking in and trapping me from within.

I hit a knot where I could not untie, I had to cut the cord and feast off it on the spot. It had me creating a new chain reaction, one where I had a fighting chance, just to fight off those demons in advance. For they were feasting off my spirit to get ahead, lining me up for another dead end.

I could sense I was building a foundation around that debt. It handed me the reservation to follow through to the next destination. Creating the wrong piece would be detrimental to my voice. I decided to move on take it all with a stride and move forward not look back while I subdivide.

I could sense I hit a dead end added with a death threat. A final review where the corrupt had its essential development. Where it saved me right through, I could feel the burden being lifted from above my shoulders, lining up between those who could see, and he who was tracing my identity.

Where my thoughts were so negative it was taking over my serenity. Where the unjust assumed continuing on that pace, will give them the power to erase and follow up on another trace. Just to keep me trapped in a world, created in my head leaving me unwrapping another gift instead.

Just so I never get ahead. What a cheap shot, I had to erase to get back on track face those who had power to cancel me out. Ghost me with doubt what a final I had to deliver then finish off while I consider the facts. Reminding myself the end was a trend the beginning of a final to hand a remedial.

No longer will they be able to feed off my spirit, so they can continue to achieve and cave in on the concept, because my method was creating a war in their piece leading them to a destination where they no longer have reservation. Lining me up for a curse I could not reverse.

Leaving me following the wrong path the one that messed up my heart. Left me spaced out from the past. Creating a better lifestyle one that will last, where I get a chance to relive my passion in advance and hold the corrupt to contempt so when I hit the last and final frontier,

I no longer live in regret or resentment. Handed a praise, for I knew within myself, there was a challenge I could defeat. Where I hit that everlasting effect created the piece that finalised that test. Track them down have the corrupt confess, corner them, by serving them another interest.

Where the only thing I get to look back on now is the last thing I started. A trace to trap reserve pauses an effect cause an energy to restore my presentation. Feeding off that temporary piece that gave me the power to release. What created the piece also stated the facts, it brought me forward.

Just to cancel out what was leading towards the wrong path. For Those who were in on it, had their eye on me and my key. Creating conflict in my path so I continue to feast off the bad news. Instead of giving me a chance to get through. A follow up on another precious moment was the clue.

It led me to another avenue, just so I can relive it, creating a piece of resistance. I was ganged up on, no one will give me a chance, when I hit my pinnacle, needed a helping hand. No one of true value was there to support me. Just the corrupt, the ones who knew and the ones who had a clue.

The only way I could state it, was recreate it, then follow up on another key. A trace I had to replace and get back on track and erase. I was pushed off the edge creating a second chance, a death threat in advance. A given chanced reverse that curse hand it back to the sender, three-fold.

Now we hit a hold up, my thumbs are up my fist in the air victory is among us. I am about to throw a flare in the air. Giving the corrupt a chance to come clean return the favour. Where my mind was made up, and my last laugh was a prank to give the unjust a chance counteract.

That free ride that I once had was a clue, where I knew if I preached my truth. I would get back on track revive another violent attack and then try to get out of that debt. The one that left me paying out with a threat, instead of trying to finalise that debt that had me tormented in the end.

Leaving me praising those who knew, having me cave in on the concept so I never get through. All while they were selling me out, sailing through innocently like they never knew. For it was entertaining them somehow and I knew I had to fight back with a backlash.

Returning to cash in, challenge the corrupt change the concept. So, when I return, I could state a fact pass a test and call it a day. For some reason, I was on the mark trying my hardest to feed off the harvest. Creating a piece and make sure when I reveal another clue, I could unravel it all.

Feed off the concept, state a fact and prevent the corrupt from ever returning. By using me to get back on track. They did my head in trying their best, to lure me back in and then create a piece to interact with my spirit, just to feed off it, on a continuous basis.

While lining me up and winding me down looking for another fight trying their luck stating a fact creating a piece returning the favour so they can release. Answering my prayers so I can find peace, part two was their vengeance part one was get a clue.

Parts three four and five will lead them to a destination of death threats and dead end. Blacklisted until the end. For keeping up with the program was a challenge I could not divide, nor subside or even follow it though because that method was based on my creativity to survive on my sensitivity.

For there was no time out to state a fact serve a sentence, create piece to give the corrupt another fighting chance to release. For they were creating a war, descending from one end to the next, where destination was an obligation towards an interrogation.

Just to cleanse clear present the corrupt with a final review. One where judging me will not get them through. Trying there hardest to score a goal, was leaving me debating what to do next. A condition I could not reveal, revive, or review until I hit the end of that journey and the beginning of anew.

Everything was costing me, it was way overdue, all I could think about was; who do I screw to get through. Unless I traced it long enough to erase it, I will have to pretend. Potent as I was, did not make a difference I was being traced trapped tricked and challenged to get in.

The corrupt were conspiring to feed off me, on the condition they had repetition. Kindly preventing me from ever reliving a competition. Where they cave in on the concept, trace those who were stalling. Giving the corrupt a chance to fall into a violent endeavour the one that harms them.

The assumption was for the corrupt had the power to repeat. Report rebel condition and scheme for another day to restore their energy, skipping another fantasy. What a hold up, where I was left shocked. I had to endure to create a presentation, that gave me the hold up I need to reserve.

Where I lost my endearment, the power to restore my anger. It had me devouring dividing and conquering a trace misplaced to put on path where I can entertain my spirit. Where I am given a chance to get through with the indication, I could follow up on another point of view.

Where I no longer lie to myself to undo an outcome that gave the corrupt power to surrender. How I return this time around will become my final review, for the concept had changed and so did the scheme of themes. For those who assumed they succeeded failed.

For they were feeding off me on a continuous basis, I could not see ahead of me. Eventually I felt the pain that was taking over my thought patterns. I knew that in the end the only way out of that dead end, was become as toxic as them. Not allowing to take the best, creating the worst of me.

I was being traced, I felt trapped in a world, not welcome. A chance to reconsider the facts in advance on how to rip my heart out. Little did they know what I knew was not a clue, it was an indication I was about to hit an alleviation. Prewarned prior, way before I had to go through it all.

Repeat report relive that point of return. where I fell out of the presentation reaching the next level with one indication, a revelation where I fell in a trap. Followed my route fed off that trace and got out freely. With no energy to replace, just a feast to accompany the corrupt for one more release.

No trace or trap left behind for the corrupt to refine, I had no time for that. It was a test to hand me that position a proposal. purely to teach me a lesson. When I reach my pinnacle, I can create a second chance. On the condition whatever I state in the mist of all evil, I can make it happen.

Where the only person to blame for that error was unjustifiable. For the individual who knew assumed he could wrap me up in cotton wool. Return whenever they wanted, consuming energy whenever they pleased, hitting the concept out of the ordinary.

Straight in to the black and blue where everything was out of place. Where the only way I could get out of that mess was create a subordinate. For they assumed I was inferior and they were way more superior than I. It led me down a path of lowering my standards, I had to recreate a new road.

Where others took me seriously, but that was far from the truth. I had several energies trying to return to bring me down and hold me hostage so they can cope copy me and then elope. By feeding me and creating a whole lot of Malarkey.

While I looked the part, I took the role too, I was terrorised by those who were trying to get in. Wondering on every level how I do what I do, and how they can get in and do it to. Listing my faults was a method where the corrupt could not wait to entertain me with an anomaly.

Apparently, I was not good enough. So, they decided to return repeat report and start an alliance. Where this time around I caused an effect restored my energy created a piece followed my path caved in on the system and returned the favour one last time.

Where the corrupt no longer have the power to repeat, report, declare a thing from me. Because I returned the favour threefold. Those vendettas that were created in my piece, was a challenge I restored just by stating a fact. Where they no longer have the power to continue to revive a dive.

Surviving on my spirit, will no longer exist nor can the corrupt persist. For they were let go long ago. I moved on created a new piece changed my perception and stated a new fact one where the corrupt will fail and no longer have the power to relocate for their life is now in the hands of God.

A hint with a mystery, where the scent was in mist it was creating a new gist. Serving me a trace that had me repeating another case. For when I go back and forth the end will no longer be pending nor will the corrupt have a chance to stand their ground again.

I hit the next round from the ground up, where the only way I could reminisce was return. Then hit the corrupt internally. Returning for a trace serving me well at the end of the race. Reclaiming the truth, hitting a test, lead me to an ending, reserving the right to accommodate that final reservation.

 An answer that had the corrupt surrendering by assuming the worst. Gave me a chance to fight back first. Before the decision was made to change my destiny, lead me on, holding onto that tribute. It failed me in the end of that trend that presented with a clue that heaved at me right through.

I had lost my, instead of failing me, it served me well. What I had was a challenge that brought me forward and presented me with a clue. I get to reserve the right to undo whatever was haunting me right through. In the end of that trend there was a made-up story the one that was holding me back.

It kept me at bay waiting for the day I could play it my way. It undid and handed me the power to push forward, breach a contract and remain silent. While the corrupt return for another yearning the one hand, I needed that handed the corrupt a chance in advance to repeat that trance.

For I got chance to make the first bid, on the edge of reason. Before the corrupt hit treason, handing me a final competition. I went back in time claimed what was owed restored my energy, and threw myself off the habitual rut, the one that gave the corrupt another chance to rot.

The offence was paid off, before they had a chance to decline. Cleared the debt with one notion in mind. That was to repair those negative thoughts, that took over my mind. Not to prepare the corrupt for dead end or death threats. Lead them towards ruins with an added pause until the End!

AMEN!

This time around my failures were nothing but a wish list to the corrupts method. It was not real all of it was created by a personal attack by he who wanted a piece of the action. Cashing in then trying to create a winning streak to those who follow up and try their luck by feeding off the concept.

All by handing me bad luck where it created a war in my piece to record my messages. Then try their luck by establishing another conspiracy attempting to relay messages. Then rely on me to do them favours. It got to the point I hit a high note, a final review to finish off the concept.

 Challenge the corrupt so I can get through. A method to see if I can condition it to my favour and record another failure to their method. Because that made up story in my head became a rude awakening. Where this time around, I found leisure to their pleasure.

Handing them a fear factor, of my own accord, was a trace I could follow up on and see if I can return the favour and hand the corrupt another feast. Those keys were mine, I earned them hit a home run by going through hard ship, there was no way I was going to share it with the corrupt.

The only way they were succeeding was by hitting me and running. Getting away with, what was about to come to fruition. It was creating energy to stall a little longer to see where they can continue to follow up on another trace and ponder to end the race sooner.

Where they assumed they could use me to predict a conflict. Creating a future event to meet there needs so they can continue to progress. Time passed and I had no point what I had was a feast about to be released. Just so I can return feed off the concept and reveal another third wheel.

Where they create a gem to that method where I finalised the key and prevented the corrupt from ever returning and using me. A turn of events that will give me the power to revive, for I was on an assignment of ousting out, their mission. While pausing an effect handing the corrupt a feast.

Meanwhile ending all inhibitions so I can continue to take pride in my work. Return at a later recreate another gamble to that feast by releasing a trap, to get them to speak the truth. A pact they cannot deny where that demon created a feast that handed me the power to release.

It was creating the wrong piece presenting me with a defamation to their allegation, so I can find peace. For that case was mine, ready to be closed because I found a way to rely on those who assume they have the power to consume. What they have is another day to resume another round.

I did not have time for that key to be wasted, for they were being prejudice to me. There was no denial or final what there was, presented me to lead, towards a destination and create a war in my piece. Handing me a follow up to the next feast while the corrupt continue to release and I persist.

Consciously feeding off me to find peace will no longer be part of the mission. For the position I am in now has overcome the corrupts deception. Where they will no longer have the power to enter my realm serve me a sentence; unless I return for a vengeance.

They tried to interact by summoning me, how entertaining they were. Assuming they could enter my world and feed whenever they please. Where I had to lie to myself long enough to trick them. When I saw joy return with no redemption. Just the hard truth and the final frontier.

Lead them to remorse, feed off the force. An indication, I was about to hit a dead end, if I did not tread carefully on that final debt. Where I get through freely no power to screw me right through. I peeked way to early and left the corrupt returning for a favour so they continue to release peace.

Where I feed of that method, facing another demon

instead. While creating anarchy, causing effects, and handing me dead ends. Relying on me to hand them a key by entering my head, was handing me information so they can continue to restore their energy and get ahead.

With the notion that I was dead, and assuming they could hit me with a dead end. Was forcing me off the edge feeding off me every time the corrupt had death threat in the head. The fact I was right on track waiting for the right moment to cause an effect, could not be wasted.

The destination changed the method, preventing the corrupt from ever recreating another event. They were in debt with me and they owed me another key. The path I was on was conditioning another song, a singular event that was failing the corrupt with every debt.

A failure to that poison that was leading me astray, it was lining me up me up for an episode. A bad day, a repetition for foul play. I had not reached my pinnacle just yet, returning the feast was failing to recreate an annulment, to that presentation leading me towards the wrong destination.

For the corrupt decided to enter my realm add more problems and worries to my woes. Where they decided to disqualify me so they can get through hit me again. Then finalise another feast to that piece, presenting me with another key. A final review to recreate a mission or two.

Where I questioned my method followed the wrong path. Restoring their energy and involving in my affairs as if I was there to feed them instead of me living my life the way it was written. It created a force a piece holding onto a past event so they can find peace. Where I had to control my anger.

It was not easy holding back when I knew the plan but I had to play it safe. The corrupt were planning a hit and run then leave me stagnant to my development all so they can continue to roam. It was extremely difficult holding back my anger took, it over; all I wanted to do was run them over.

So, I decided to bite the bullet take a punch not except a bribe unless I benefit. Enough with the delegating and the energy wasting. I had to refine refuse and create an everlasting due. Hand them a dose of their own medicine while I corner them with a trace I cannot replace.

After the way I was treated by those who were returning to repeat it. They were asking for trouble; asking for favours for they had me hit me and ran left me violent to. Warning me if I did not play it their way, I would get arrested. For they were on a second trial a third and a final revival.

Where this time around, I get to reveal another key the one I steal from them, so I can survive another deal. It was my turn to press delete delay and pray to God they never progress or succeed in their endeavours. Because they hit me and ran leaving me suffering in silence so they succeed.

Another hit and run, was challenging me in the long run, I had to overcome another outcome that did not serve me well. While creating the piece I needed to release for that poison was the corrupts method to revived and accommodate another survival technique.

So, when they return for another hit and run the outcome will work to my favour, and we are done. Now that I am on the cusp of creating a piece, overcoming a test, and moving on like I did not lose a thing. Giving me the power from within to gain the wisdom I need to win.

For I was constantly on the run, I could not sit in one place, the anxiety was killing me from within, I felt out of place. I was fighting off my demons that were actually mind reading me from within. It felt as if I was fighting a lost cause, keeping me failing every race so they can win.

I needed to find peace, sit still, and recreate a feast to those who were attaching themselves to my spirit. While that etheric chord kept them balanced, I was not at ease. I felt it with such pressure it was harming me. I was trying my hardest to harvest and find peace.

I knew there was a toxic energy surrounding me, it connected to my synergy. Somewhat leaving me stagnant to my conscious awareness, releasing a feast and finalising another piece. All so I can get back on track and face my demons with ease and terrorising them as I continue to peak.

When I became aware of what was really happening, I decided to take another approach. Restoring my energy as I continued to grow. Was leaving me personally attacking the corrupt final revelation. For I knew I was being stalked by those who want to feed.

Where this time around, I found a way in to cash in and continue my path. Cleaning up the mess before they caved in on me and tried to get me to compress. For, they were not going to confess, but they were going to challenge me with a finally that had me reliving another anomaly.

A destination providing me with conformation so I never proceed. Just to cleanse my spirit, feed off that reservation, get back on track and repeat another fact. What a conundrum I fell into just to find myself and remind myself; I was living a lie to cover up the truth, so I can get by.

CHAPTER 10

◆ ◆ ◆

WHO EVER MADE ME SEE IT!
ALL SO MADE ME STATE IT

They would not let it go, unless I stalled, traced trapped and fed off that pace. It handed me the condition to erase a competition. I fell into a trap of releasing a vision for, I knew I had followers everywhere trying to arch me up so they can continue to feed off me. Because they were corrupt.

Release a perception that held me to redemption, created. A follow up to the next composition determined to keep up with the programme, where I was allowed to return then trace it then undo another piece to that feast. Where my outlet was to create a piece to bring peace.

There were certain individuals who assumed they were more powerful than I. Competing with me was the only way they could get by. I was not aware of my capabilities;

I hit a hold up because of it. Sitting in the middle of a trace waiting for the ending to embrace stuck surrendering another case.

Trying there hardest to have me harvest, the wrong end, to make me a victim again. Where they decided to create another fight on the hope they can get in and finalise a hit then run. With one indication that was to follow up to the next destination.

It left me terrorised by an outcome, for they assumed they had more energy to consume. Because they had more man power than I. All I had was a refuge to review a trace refuse the corrupts phase and finalise that case. A feast to erase and prepare me for another case; one I can relate too

Where I had to return cancel, condition, and repeat another vision. Where this time around I do not hand internal bliss what I hand is the Abys. A foundation I wish not to reminisce. For the curse had been reversed and the presentation was to release another revision, to my mission.

Just to give in to that threat that was causing a neglect. It was caving in on the concept so I can get back on track and create a co-dependency; to those who had energy by feeding off me. For the turn of events gave me the power to return, close one door and open another, so I can further.

Because I had several stalking me, waiting for me to fail it was freeing me. With another passive aggressive approach to the next sail. Just so they can attempt to take over my key. Then restore their energy. It got to the point I had to trace trap follow my route, and not look back.

On the condition I get my point across. For those who attacked me in the end will spare me the drama. They will look at life, dislike the dream and dramatize for what they caused on my end was already finalized. Where now we are no longer friends not even enemies until the end

In the end I am done pretending I am their friend. Keeping up with the program while creating war in my piece will no longer bring them peace. It will backfire and you will end up dead to the bone buried before there time I have moved on I am done peaking and pleasing the corrupts outcome.

Keeping me closer now will give them dead ends and death threats. My presence brought serenity but the corrupt made so many errors where my presence was repairing the damages. By creating a challenge in the vicinity of those who were silent.

For they created the wrong piece, just so they can feed off the method. In turn sent me packing, before I had a chance to restore my energy in advance and release peace. Assuming they had the power in numbers to face me and make my light less bright all so they continue to feed off me.

Repeating a dead end added with spite. Lucky for me I had no time or freedom to pretend but I did have a presentation and I was ready to reveal a divination and this time around I have revivification. My creativity was cut short before they had a chance to state a new fact.

because I found a way to restore my energy feed of the present take advantage of those who knew and validate another clue. They thought they could use me to get a clue advance and create another anomaly right through by attempting to line me up with another dead end.

Those who met me half way took me for a fool and ran off like they had the power to feed off the mission. Run hide divide and conquer another vibe while leaving me depleted by attacking my vision. Leading me on, leaving creating a proposition to give the corrupt composition.

Personally, attacking my spirit feeding off my energy creating a war in my peace. Where I was stating the facts and repeating another trace to that pace. Plotting to see how to feed off me and my, talents as I was, on the trace creating another feast restoring my energy to release peace.

All so I can continue to develop and find peace. Because my method had it lists and the only way, I could persist is by creating the Abys. I had no trace or the vision to erase, I had to follow up on a path. Uncover up on another deception and return the favour by retaliating.

Then handing the corrupt redemption, all while I was undoing another revelation. What I had was a competition, lining me up for revision, to plan out another foundation to create a new route. Where my feet hit the ground and my head all clouded by the system, was redeeming that energy.

Safe and sound, reliving the drama no longer and that key that was stolen from me, returned. Without the repetition to lead the corrupt towards a destination and hand them destruction. What was to come next, was a final request an entity with no regret.

because of the environment I was in was more than I thought it was a dead end where I realised, I was being put through another test again. A test of endurance, a chemical reaction to prepare me for the next destination, for their alchemist was out of whack.

He could not state a fact or create a piece without me, for his peripheral vision was being tarnished. Handing him confidential information was no longer part of the trace.

He was way to strong back then. I did not play the game that was handed to me it was amended by he who caused it.

I decided to turn against him, that was the only way I could live through another bad day. Avoid a problem, where it had me holding onto a curse where I could not reverse. Unless I praised those who knew and assumed they hit me with another clue; there was no turning back, no time for that.

What another personal vendetta I had to skip, just to find a day to condition. Feed off the mission and create another repetition. Where I get to state my facts create my piece and get served. For what is owed to me will be another predicament where I get a chance in advance to follow my path.

Advance and not reveal another loss. Because whatever was stated was also on the long and short. A side effect I could not restore, a narrative to give me the inner power to return the favour. A condition where the mission, held me back so I can get back on track and create an evolution.

Handing me the power and the interrogation, reveal confess another distinction. I Just need to relay those messages. While bringing them forward. all while I was restoring my energy. It was giving me the power to attempt another solitude, because they could not threaten or harm me here.

I was way past it, returning purely to steal that view, before it came to fruition. if it worked in there favour it would become detrimental to society. I was way too ahead of them though, I locked it in faked another death to lure them away, then press replay.

Once I conditioned it to my favour, I returned, any time there was no time frame. Finalise another crime. Where there was no other case to reconsider, because I traced trapped challenged the corrupts repetition, recreated a piece where I can challenge the corrupt to release peace.

Case close and reveal another revision, for that key that was created was a safety net. Where I get back on track relay, release that debt. Putting the corrupt through hell, so I can find peace. Just so I can return the favour face my fear and solemnly swear that their method will never cease.

For it was created by peace and they were returning for war to give me the energy to harm myself once more. It led me to a destination where I was misinformed, following the wrong path was the only way I can reenlist, create another restoration to that elimination.

Where I no longer need reassurance, or list the faults of others to get through. Warning them to keep their distance was a challenge I could not reform. Recreate or even get them to salivate. For every time I came across that meet, I fell into a trap of dead ends and death threats.

Lining me up for a fight, was a method where the corrupt assumed they had the power to resume and keep me silently supressing, while they were processing towards thew next progress. It gave me the indication I was on the right path and the reason, retaliating for treason.

For they assumed I was not established, in fact I was preestablishing, Finalising everything. When they figured it out, they came out, ready to reserve the right to conserve, releasing another serve. Personally, attacking me, made them feel superior, in the end it served me a sentence.

Brought me forward gave me a chance to go back in time and create a new break. It was part my birth right, I was not to lose hindsight, even though I lost my way I was not to lose another day. Because my challenges were just a test to recreate another contest.

For others who knew could not wait to get through it belted the hell out of me. Just so they can find solitude all the way. Trying my hardest to trace trap and trick the corrupt into another threat. As a treat a mission accomplished, for I had no regret. It had sent me down a path of repeating a cut.

My gut feeling was warning me I was about to hit with another catastrophe. The vision had me interpreting the corrupts trace, a trap to condition the mission, get back on track. Giving in, was the only way I could consider returning the favour, at a final date, relay messages then turn the pages.

Not giving them a chance to repeat report or retaliate, to pause effects. The last thing I wanted was to lose my way, finalise that trace all the way. Considering the facts, I was concentrating on getting back on track. A feast that had me preserving them, and preventing me from reliving a dream.

The tragedy began it gave the corrupt a head start. What they had was no use to them what they had was I on the loose. Only then what happened in-between was nowhere near where things were meant to be. For all I knew I was being used abused and left to suffer in between.

Until I gave in to the corrupts mind reading gamble, I was left to undo that final review. Relive that drama, losing the one thing that had me repeating another inning. A sacrament from the beginning. Where the end was not as reserved for a dead end but a challenge where I can feed of their success.

For there to many fights and no momentum, or ammunition to write a wrong passageway. Just a final review to keep strong. Entering the unknown, was the only way to condition the mission. Then and continue my path, for what I knew now and what I was meant to do to look beyond the now.

A line up between the here the now, was near where I was to get through and hell broke loose. So did the method that served the corrupts debt. The one that ended up becoming a good deed in the end. Because the corrupt were on the path of pretending, I was not going to live past my prime.

For I was on the path of repeating a challenge, where this time around; what a round up. I was not going to miss another boat, nor give the corrupt a chance to evoke or provoke another fight. Where I could spread the news, waste no more time following a path that had no ending in sight.

For it was a never-ending story, that failed me. I was constantly whinging and whining about the past for the present validated a question mark. For X marked the spot in the end, and at the back of my mind, wondering where did I go wrong, how to continue my path and keep strong.

In the heat of the moment, I created a piece violently stating a fact just to get back on track and counteract another pact. Relaying messages to those who knew put them through hell. Just so I can get through, that presentation that was holding me back creating a fact back-to-back.

Those who were conspiring to cause an effect. Were giving me a chance in advance to reject their method. For they took me for a fool releasing a negativity towards my direction. What a passive aggressive approach I had to cave in on. Just to get the final manifestation to the next destination.

Where I decided to retaliate, in a way that will hand me a key to get back on track. Not allow them to return and challenge me. For those who restored the energy, also created a piece to feast off. Those who assumed they had power to release, feed of that trace get back on track, will state a fact.

For they will no longer have the power to cause an effect. Case close or create a foreclosure, for it was the only way I can undo another bad day. Returning for a feast from a past event, was a challenge I tried to prevent, it led me to a destination where the only way in was the way out.

Where they can find peace, try to compete condition, and meet half way with repetition. While repeating another termination. It was a challenge I did not want to participate with, because I knew if I gave in that method was a praise, to hand me a condition to feed off the mission.

For the corrupt assumed they can return whenever they pleased. Causing a problem state a fact release another feast. For there was no way I was coming back for a gamble, and give those who assume they have the power to consume, scam me with another scheme.

Because that test created a piece left me finalising another feast. Returning now will be purely for me to plant a seed. Retrieve and achieve my goals mentally emotionally and physically. Make sure next time, I reach my potential it will be on my terms and conditions not theirs.

So, I can have my cake eat it too and no longer justify my actions to you know who. When I catch up with those who conspire I can turn it around to my favour and release another demon. where I can condition and hand the corrupt a repetition added with definition to their mission.

Having said that, I had to override another siren, and provide the corrupt with a dead end. While I contrate and not lose focus, or faith a challenge with its own reward. Because I moved in to a place where I fell out of place, No one was giving me a chance to redeliver or contaminate.

Just confirm the result, then undo what I knew creating a conflict between the two. Based on a trace that had me negative, reliving my destiny again. A praise to erase a past figure release that demon that served me in the end of that measure. Where I had no time out to follow up on another phase.

The feast was too hard to release, nor track me down. Trying my luck to create a piece, was way to profound. Where I was given a chance to get back on track releasing peace. Fell in a trap of a dead ends constantly being rejected, took its toll. It presented me with a huge fortune in my mission.

All so I can release another piece and fast forward to the next feast. Casting a spell, casing those who had it in for me and then trying my luck to see if I can return and hit them back with bad luck. The only way I could follow through undo and try my hardest to, was turn, corner, trace another feat.

While I get in repeat and regain consciousness in between. Find a way to reject them too, so I can end the race sooner and get through. Because that trace was a follow up to the next race the only way to return the favour was undo and no longer concentrate on another failure.

Divide and conquer and mind read those who were given me a hard time and cut them out completely so I can continue to climb. No time than the present, to fight back and feed off the pressure that led me to a destination where my freedom was given a final review.

The only way to return the favour was save myself from another failure. I could sense the corrupt were coming back to repeat and this time round they were warned, if they state it again the whole concept will be torn and they will no longer have power to retrace or follow up on another case.

In the end of the race the force will embrace handing e the power to return undo then devour another clue. There was no trace or race to end, I completed my tasks before they had a chance to re-enter and pretend. I surrendered, moved on took the energy I needed to restore a theme.

The pathway I was meant to follow before I was side tracked. Led to believe that the dream was mine. I was grooming another without my consent. Time, I returned repeated it, put that individual back where they started no freedom or time out just a dead end, every time they hit a friend.

A past event that nearly had me reliving a dead end. The path I was on made no difference to the game I knew I had to retrace recall. Cave in on the concept and made sure the corrupt fail and fall in a trap of repetition. Not get out until they hand me what they owe me, without assigning another.

I was way out, moved on, found opportunity to hit and run, milking it for all its glory. The debt was set in cement, that had not set yet. Nor did it have a set time as long I live the task completed by me. If I do not complete it will end with me, until the grave, even then, the repeat will be mine.

There were no mistakes misshaped or problems. However, the corrupt assumed they could enter my realm forge my signature and finalise a crown. It got to the point I had no time for them, but I played it purely to return the favour clear the debt and feed off the method so I can get back on track.

While I resurrect and repent, waiting for the corrupt to give in, I decided too way them down. Warn them in and hand them a challenge creating a collage in between. Hitting an ending that was pending giving me the power I needed to surrender devour from within lining me up so I can win.

Not only win the concept but another competition. Where if they return later, it will hand me a challenge I can reinstate and take the gamble I need to preach and get through without losing another clue, because the game was a scam to keep me down, kick me out.

Leading me to a destination with hatred, doubt; short and sweet. A scheme for another day to convey. Lead the corrupt to a destination where they have no bay, no choice but to give in and hand me everything. Because they preyed on me hit me, ran, and left me suffering in the long run.

When I hit the pinnacle, before they had a chance to remain vigilant to the game. I took a gamble finalised another scam, recreated a piece to give me a chance to release and find peace. Because that creation was a lie for me to get by, I decided to write a wrong and call it a day.

While I curse the momentum and find a way to free myself from another bad day. Call it a free ride to the other side a follow up on a signature momentum. A foundation I could not feast or praise because the vision was a competition to release a key.

To finalise a presentation to cough up what was stolen off me. I did not give in the way it was stated or give way. because I was way too emotional to play it their way. I played it the way I felt feasible for they were irresponsible cursing my every challenge by feeding me lies and deception.

I knew I was being conned, I just could not prove it and the only way I could solve was stir the pot. Cause an effect create a piece and have them serve a sentence so I can release peace. Even though I finished with honours, I had way too many tribulations and obstacles.

Where I had others trying their luck playing the game of pot luck. Restoring my energy was the only way I can return get back on track; play a game of truth and dare. Where if I was not careful, I will end up gambling it all away, and handing the corrupt another chance to press replay.

When I reached my limit, I took the initiative, followed my route. Even tormented those who had given me the indication of regret and self-doubt. I was way hard on myself and the only way I could entrap was trick the corrupt to get back on track it handed them a trip down memory lane.

Then confuse them just long enough to return and refuse them. Whatever they were bullying me about, I knew they were trying there hardest to hold me up. Keep me hostage so they can steal a key leave me delaying, deleting a trace. Where I embark on another feast as I create the peace.

For I knew some how they were returning for a yearning, creating a war in my piece. It was enough for me to witness I hit another feast. When I returned from the old journey,

I walked into a drama, a nightmare where the only way I could create a piece was return the favour and save myself.

A presentation where I could hold onto that piece, follow up on another feast. Where the past response will stir the pot feed off the mission get back on track, revealing another competition. I could sense I was being tracked down, by someone who knew assuming I was his possession.

Just to cover up another clue, in fact, I was his obsession, where I could not get out fast enough. He kept luring me back in, just to feed off my win. Then he found interesting feeding off the concept. Where I was stuck again because he broke my wing took control and fed off me whole.

Push me in the corner, hit me with a trace trapping me in the end of that case. All it did was give me a chance to release and find peace. For he kept clipping at my feathers poisoning my spirit, so he can continue to repeat, compete, and hand my key to someone who was willing to replay, a gamble.

I was given the all clear and a chance repeat too then retrace and report another clue. feed off the mission as I find revision, constantly restoring my energy. So, I can find my way through prepare myself for another clue then hand the corrupt a chance to review.

CHAPTER 11

◆ ◆ ◆

RETURN THE FAVOUR WHEN NO ONE ELSE WILL! RELIGHISHING ANOTHER SPELL

While I took that beating, there was no comparison. I gave myself a chance to restore my energy in advance. I found myself in a tugger war, locked up in a second bribe. This time around I got in, raised awareness, the energy that was feeding off me, lined me up for another dead end.

Where it left me considering pulling the string. Lucky for me I had spirit, caving in on me. It saved me that is when I knew I was on the path to recovery. Leaving the corrupt finalising another variation to that destination, handing me the realization, I hit another hold up, so I can return, clear the debt.

My name to that game was tarnished it created a mass murder. Making sure the corrupt get punished for repeating another bad day. For they had a chance to cheat chase me then press delete on the condition. I continue to feed off the mission, hand them a presentation.

Just to help them validate another deception. Where the only way I could find repetition, was return the favour creating an outcome. Just to cause an effect and cave in on the concept. Then resurrect with the notion, I prevent the corrupt from ever returning the favour.

The test was a side effect, that gave me the power to disinfect. I had to defer before, I had a chance to repeat and press delete. For I did not have enough information to uncover up another reservation. Nor refine and follow up on a trace to get back on track and erase.

I was trapped in a world reliving another nightmare, a life style that created a war. Where I was taken for a ride a trip down memory lane, to continue my mission. For those who compete compel and try to complete a mission on my jurisdiction were about to get a taste of their own proposition.

They took the wrong approach, a final feast to return, look, see if they can repeat another key. To turn those events that was creating the piece against me, it created the feast that listed the faults that made that method way more refined. became a constant repetitive thought.

Where the only way, I could state the facts was return the favour and hit them back. Approaching the end of a bad start is now on the mend. I caused an effect created a piece and fell out of that trap that handed me an amendment another fleet with dead end with death traps.

I was constantly on the go, I had nowhere to go, my foundation was to collapse with a no show. I was about to relapse a fact, where this time around I created a piece. Followed up on another trace, then side tracked. Starved by those who fighting to keep the corrupts fire burning.

I had to return, state a fact, burn the pages, and pass the test. All while I handed the corrupt another free ride. Towards a destination where they cannot combine with mine. I returned and tore their behind. They were it in it to win it, their assumptions were to create a war in my piece, repeating it.

Finalising another feast, because they knew it all, if they had powers to report and review another clue. In the end it was enough for me to see I was on the right path where I had to do recondition and get back on track and repeat it.

Revealing a vampire effect, to test the patience of those who resurrect. Was a warning that someone was out to steal my identity creating an anomaly in my piece to finalise a review. Assuming they had the power to accommodate another hold up, disrespecting my every move then facing me.

All friendly; as if they did nothing to harm me. In fact, they started a fight, took me in listed my faults and trapped me with a second chance, to pretend. All so they can get a chance to get in and feed off me from within. That method violated the truth, it led me to a destination where I had to fight back.

Then reveal another clue. Where several who knew used my method to help themselves. Meanwhile feeding off me, where I had to retaliate return and undo the damage. The one that was done to me right through. It created a piece, where those who knew used me and took me a fool.

It gave others the indication I was easy and they could feed off me too. It created a spiral effect of negativity. I could not fight off unless I projected it too and lead them to a destination of the dead ends and death threats right through. I was on the move hitting a final then when the time come;

God knows! All I knew to continue that method, I had to reveal another clue. Lure them in, give them what they want. Then when the time come lead them astray, when they least expect it. Return, turn it around finalise that outcome to my favour. On the hope I condition the mission.

Failing the corrupts vision, on the hope I get the response I needed to skip another clue. Revive that method so I can get back on track and survive another feast. The one where I can cash in flush it without fail and release peace. I fell into a trap of leads indicating I was losing, in fact, I was winning.

Where the corrupt could see, I was working on me, succeeding with a high degree. The more I tried the better I become and the harder they became on me. They turned against me, where I had no freedom to recreate reveal or even state a fact to contaminate the corrupts hunt on my name.

So, I can get back on track and retake control of my destiny. I had so many obstacles to overcome they repeated it with an outcome. Where I had no freedom to pretend or descend all I had was another day to comprehend, where I went wrong and how to fix it in the long run.

Defending my honour was one method, I could not follow up on too soon. I had to take the initiative and my time to cash in and validate another window to opportunity. I did not want to lose another chance to finalise my spirit in advance. For my foundation had its validation.

Where those cracks in the concrete were normal, and I knew patching it up to soon will give the corrupts chance to get through. I had to go back in time find out what was holding me hostage and undo it as I conduit. A condition to Cancel them out it was the only way I could state a fact.

By creating a position to help me get back on track, finalising that trace to my favour. Returning the favour created a revelation to hand me the position. The one I needed to get that revision and hand the corrupt composition, for I knew the path I was on, was a competition.

Where I assumed I was shoe in but in fact I was feeding those who were competing, so I decided to feed off that to and hand those who were looking for answers to compete with me. A challenge where the competition was restoring me energy handing me revision.

I was not aware of gave me the trace, I needed to create a better awareness. Just to startle those who assume they power in number to consume. In my peripheral vision, I started to take notice I was being watched by a sasquatch, constantly in the corner of my eye.

Waiting for me to uncover another lie and every time I did there he was; Waiting for me to challenge my spirit so he can be free. All while, I would look back meet him eye to eye facing my fear. Where he would run and disappear in the woods where my third eye would switch off.

While I look back disorientated by the constant pursue. It felt way to persuasive to cancel out and get through. But perusing, and refusing to let it go had me confused by the whole turn of events. It created a silent siren in between here there and everywhere.

I knew if I did not stop looking for that creature my life would not be worth living. I would hit a dead end creating a death threat all over again. Handing the living dead, a chance to steal another feast. Just to that piece, adding negative thoughts in the end, where I had to let go and set it free.

What a challenge I had to release to find peace, retrace that divination. Reveal another confirmation to my destination. I knew I had to divide and conquer a momentum, that left me silently pretending. I was skipping another preservation to create a piece to harm the corrupt.

Right at the end of the mission, during the transition. For every time they hit a hold-up, it stirred the pot. For there was no indication that I had a free ride to rewrite my manuscript. It was a lie just to give the corrupt a chance to close the deal in advance, all it did was took them for a ride.

Handing me a key, taking whatever, they could, no longer resuming. Allowing me to catch up and catch them in the act undoing every clue. For that someone who knew, thought he had all the answers. For he was lucky enough to live through and experience my journey in advance.

A challenge after the next, had no meaning nor a final request. That was before I was pulled out of unworthy debt. For he had a personal request, he assumed he was my personal guest. In fact, he was an intruder and damn good one. He had many acquaintances and the finances to back him up.

He could conspire with any one for he was corrupt.

Inspiring them to see what makes my spirit create energy, where I click and return to reveal another fluke. Sparing the drama that was about to follow. The truth will provide me the substance, the sustenance to release a certain thought wave.

I was stating a fact and making sure when I hit back, I get back on track without losing my royalties. I was surrounded by way too much disloyalty. All so, I can restore my energy and feed off the method that send me down a black hole full of deep and sorrowful thoughts of toxicity.

Where I was about to lose hindsight of reality and my creativity. Handing it to an individual who was feeding off me just to find a new lease in a life. If I gave in to early and handed the corrupt another chance to divide and conquer, they would have done my head in even longer.

Having me chase away a dream, that was not a pipe one, in fact it was all in the book. I was on the path to make it real and they knew and tried sabotage it and call it an obstacle. Where they could not wait to repeat follow me everywhere, try their luck to silently erupt causing an effect.

Stir the pot by taking the plunge and damaging my spirit so they can continue to rummage. For they knew what ever was set by me would, become a precedent eventually. It was a phase though a class act to give the corrupt another chance to condition a vision in advance.

A method that gave me the power to rely on he who created the piece and tried their luck to release. Returning to finalise another hand out. Handing me bad luck, a key to bring me forward trace trap an envision another mission about to relapse.

Prepare me now for another challenge, for I am

experienced here. I have learnt my lesson met my match hit a siren. Even created a piece of my own to teach the corrupt not to mess with the mission. because I made it the next proposal my hardship was based on reliving a dream.

Creating a nightmare in between, for those who knew and those who had a clue were courageous. I decided to let it go and create a new vision. One where I can mix and match, live my life the way it was written. Assuming hitting me and running will give them the power to recreate another drama.

The presentation to lead me towards a dead-end proposal. For they thought they were given permission by whoever had vision to swim in my pool. Cleansing their spirit so they can continue to flourish feeding off my soul. With violation giving them the power to discern and return later.

Caving in on the mission had me debating what end to take what finale to partake. If it was not for my spirit that faint heart would not feint. I will be fighting a lost cause, trouble spreading my wings, afraid to speak my truth. Stuck in a dilemma of creating a feast.

Giving the corrupt a chance to release, leaving me consolidating with he was considering the worst. Losing face value and hope because others had the power to evoke. I was not level headed either, I was stuck in Hiatus mode struck by the notion that I had division but in fact I was on a mission.

I could not stop until I completed it. Spacing out was a sense of relief, for I needed to dream a little to make the dream a reality. I was creating a nightmare in the middle of it all. Instead releasing the piece, and enjoying the outcome

I kept falling in out of traps.

Failing and feeling afraid to take the plunge, for every time I did, I would be caught up in a web of lies. Waiting for the right moment to clear the debt and move on like I had no threat. I was peaking, releasing toxicity turned by the events that gave me the indication I was about to drown in sorrow.

Instead of spreading my wings. Following my path, was a chore I was dispersing falling into a trap of dead ends, for those who were in on it were pretending to be my friend. Used my presence to cash in get back on track and win everything. I was left tracing and developing another position.

Tracing the facts give the corrupt provision. Caving in on concept, pausing effects giving the corrupt another chance in advance to release a demon. Then hand the corrupt a chance to reflect. I was being Emotionally blackmailed; terrorised by what could have been instead of what it.

It was preventing me from reliving my destiny. I felt, the pain the torture, the trace that came with it. I could sense a way out, but I had to be vigilant think quick be creative, not allow them to return. and harm me again by hammering me in the head like they did back then.

Leaning towards a destiny that gave me the power, challenges I need to free myself from a path. Where I could not see unless I return and bribed them too. All so they can get ahead finalise a death threat. What a challenge I had to prevent to give in, put a dent to the corrupts energy.

That preventative measure became a free ride, I got a chance to re-enter and subdivide. It was establishing a new beginning so I can get by and no longer lie to myself.

Because my start was a good one, that is what sent out the positive vibe, that sent chills down my spine.

Where I can come and go as I please, trace erase and finalise another piece. Accepting my honour no longer feeling defeated while I release PEACE. I was heaving holding back trying not cause more havoc. Because those who were in on it were trying there hardest to create a war in my piece.

Returning the favour would be a waste of time for there were many who were part of that system. Trying there hardest to rebuild around my energy. Feeding off me by pushing me off edge. A sense of death threats. A decision to let it go now, I knew who was in on it, and who created the piece.

Then who tried to recall, while I traced another feast to that piece. It gave me the energy to release. Not only did I manage to swindle my way out of a horrible situation, but I out lived that individual that was plotting to harm me, creating a piece nasty one to say the least.

Where he assumed he could manipulate the situation, by creating a feast to reprimand. Leave me destitute, returning the favour, refining another clue. Just to cash in and cave in on the concept, then get a second chance to rekindle a relationship, then restore the situation by repeating it.

Clearing the pathway to serenity, completely an aware that the journey was based on a trace of truth and dare. While I was making my mark, marking the spot with my signature. Ready willing and able to stir the pot, and make it happen I could sense the corrupt challenging me in another fight.

Just so I never get there. Waiting to see which end to repeat hit me and run and call it a fun run. Creating a sacrament to that rule and leaving me guessing wrong so they can continue their path and consume. Returning the favour was a challenge I could not rely on; For I knew I hit a tie.

With he who knew and he who wanted to steal that clue. Leave me gambling it all so they can get through. I had to return at a later, redo, then undo a follow up to another turn of events. Because my presentation at the beginning was a dead end. I could sense I was being torn in two worlds.

 A free ride to the other side and the other where I went through the whole nine yards. Hitting a brick wall fighting my way through either way what can I say both methods left me astray lining myself up for another bad day. It was a trace, trap that gave me the energy to return and rebuild.

For the power to reclaim my thoughts again make sure the corrupt never have trust. Trace to restore reveal or even accommodate another feast to that piece. I found them easy, somewhat conditioned by the past the present, future events. Giving me the power to prevent them from entering again.

Presenting me with a final evaluation, while I return and undo another debt. While I get the corrupt to evacuate, for my return was stagnant, I just was not there yet. Now that I am here made it to a place, I can recreate a piece a feast to feed an army.

What can I say the energy that created the piece caused the effects. Made sure when I reached my pinnacle I can retaliate. Restoring my energy and reconcile no longer, while sitting in denial, then condition it to my favour. Holding onto to one more case, a chance to open then shut that case.

What I witnessed was not what I was expecting, it nearly ended in tragedy. For I was living the lie about to trade in my light trying to get by. Where the waiting game was about to gamble my life away. If I did not give in, my life would not be worth living.

Shutting the case completely was no longer final, nor part of the task. I got to relive a trace that cased closed, long ago. No looking back wasting time allowing the corrupt to erase the crime. Attempting to cause a nasty effect was reversed, my path was deceiving the corrupts demeanour.

I instantly deleted delayed denied them access all the while l left them suffering. Planting a seed to condition that venture to work to my favour. So, when I return for the incur, it will be based purely on my condition. Where I compete compel and win every vision even the one with a final division.

The dead will no longer hold me back for that free ride to the other side was a condition. It gave me the power to control and devour. Now that I have hit my Kingdom of Heaven, earned my crown, I no longer return to hand the corrupt a day to yearn or share my values with those who condition it.

For my forthcoming event was incoming, I found inconclusive task. To turn the corrupt against one another, because the corrupt were intrusive. There method was no longer forthcoming, I changed those predictions defended my honour and created another survival technique.

A mind reading force, a torch that blew out, where I grew up and saw the world to what it was. Where I was proposed a challenge prospered to forward, to make it happen. When I got there instantly abandoned. It took my power I had to repeat and rebel against those who hit me and ran.

I took my power back when I witnessed it all for, he who had the power gave in. Assuming he had victory in the end. But I woke up from that deep sleep fought back reached my potential and got back on track. With an idea I return for a vendetta where this time around my return is like no other.

Where I will reach higher further than my potential restoring my energy and reclaim my synergy. where dropping me will here will give me the power to give in and bathe in their melody. Leaving toxicity behind there tranquillity restoring my energy every time I hit a failed formality.

For they took me on a ride, watched me suffer deeply inside. When I fell it took me on a ride to the other side. Where I survived another division, a decade of inconclusion to their diversion. Competing no longer with the underworld who undervalued me took me on a ride manifesting.

I gave in outcasted them from within for the freedom they handed me was a challenge. It was purely to pretend and leave unworthy. Knowing now what I knew then has now come to an end dispersed delivering that everlasting curse. giving the power to converse and serve them a sentence.

As I catch them in the act of kindness, waiting for that trace to come to fruition. When the time come, I return purely for one reason; treason, a happy medium. Then frame them once again, for returning for a yearning, where come first, lining them up for a dead end in the end.

Where victory will become my friend.

Amen

To be continued!

ABOUT THE AUTHOR

Panagiota Makaronis

I have a Master's degree in Philosophy and Theology from ACU Australian Catholic University. I also have a diploma in Clinical Hypnotherapy from Sterling Institute and The Australian Academy of Hypnosis.

My studies included Psychology, Neurolinguistic Programming, Meditation, and Spirituality. Over the years I have worked with many clients where I delved into Mediumship Clairvoyancy Astrology Numerology Reiki and Crystal Healing.

You name it I studied it.

I also studied the Key of Solomon which was a path I will never forget, learning that method gave me a path to Heaven on Earth! What can I say, that was an interesting concept. A hell forsaking one too!

I was on a mission of oppression, to study the human mind

and see in hindsight what makes people in society click.

I was so interested in Anthropology and Sociology, I had a lot of questions unanswered, so I decided to follow a path of the unknown to see how I can make sense of my reality.

My clients were, experimental to me I was on a mission to investigate human nature and I met a lot of interesting people along the way.

Because I was quite accurate in my craft, I had several who became quite defensive and could not wait to cover up their mess by challenging me, because they assumed I had a knowing and they could delete and delay me.

That made my life quite interesting it helped me with my writing. I had adventures where I could sense I was on a path of defending my honor while others were hiding behind the truth. Lucky for me I felt that I was being protected by my spirit along the way the Guidance from within never led me astray.

I had to take an absence of leave, because of family commitments, I went on a Sabbatical, decided to go back to university get my degree, clear my path, and bring myself back to reality.

I was fighting a lost cause living another person's life, which lead me towards a destination where I could no longer lie to myself.

During my absence of leave, I went on a path of journalism and freelance writing, I have my own blog on Facebook where I write inspirational pieces. Basically to broaden my Horizon, and to warn those who are inspired by the truth to set it all free and believe.

Not only in yourself but in life, because life is too short, My Philosophy is not to follow others or worry about what others think neither. In the end, you have to live within yourself. Face your fears and trust your instincts. Because no one really knows what is around the corner.

No one knows unless you stick to the plan and even then, your world can collapse, and you have to start again. I should know! I have passed several paths, where my foundation was not strong enough to hold me, and it would collapse where I would have to rebuild again.

What a catastrophe!

Having said that, time does not stand still, time is of the essence. Based on how much you can achieve in one lifetime, just leave a Legacy Behind.

I strongly believe you must follow your path and how it might look to others it should not matter as long as you can accept who you are then anything is possible.

Where in the end I believe the right presentation will lead you to the right destination if you persevere.

AMEN

THE THEATRICAL MELODIA OF MY LIFE

This book is based on my journey, the roller coaster I call life, my thought patterns my experiences. How I overcome so many turmoil's, how it changed my perception, for it led me towards a destination that gave me tension, where I felt I had no freedom or free will, all I had was failure, added with faith, and the hope to overcome another fall. Feeding off the concept as I rise above it all!

The Sacred Mysteries Of The Unholy Grail: The Theatrical Melodia Of My Life Part 3

This Book is the continuation, part 3 to the series of The Theatrical Melodia of my Life, a Revelation, a trial and error where I had to come up with an idea, to clear the air. Making sure my dream became a reality, that is when the stagnation and terror began and I knew I hit a final revelation.

The Key To The Chronicle Of Thanatos : Chronicle 4

The Key to the Chronicle of Thanatos is the continuation of my Manuscript, The Theatrical Melodia of My Life, KREA PREA!

A series of self-help books based on my journey and how I survived it. A journal built, around my thoughts and my Premonitions, where I had visions.

It had put me on a challenge and several wild Goose chases, just to reclaim and retain information. Those experiences took me on a path where I had to overcome certain tribulations and threats.

The Revelation To Those Who Solemnly Swear: Chronicle 5

The Revelation to those who Solemnly Swear Chronicle 5, is the continuation of my Series of the Theatrical Melodia of my Life, based on those who believe in themselves follow their pride and salvage their soul to get there.

What can I say, life is what it is, and I only know what I am capable of, for when you are aiming and achieving goals you will come across many who pass through who want to harm you.

Leading you in the wrong direction, framing you at every resurrection lining you up for a dead-end destination, all by making you believe there helping you. They are the ones that hold you, hostage, on the condition they feed off you by feeding you malarky.

www.ingramcontent.com/pod-product-compliance
Lightning Source LLC
Chambersburg PA
CBHW021237090426
42740CB00006B/571